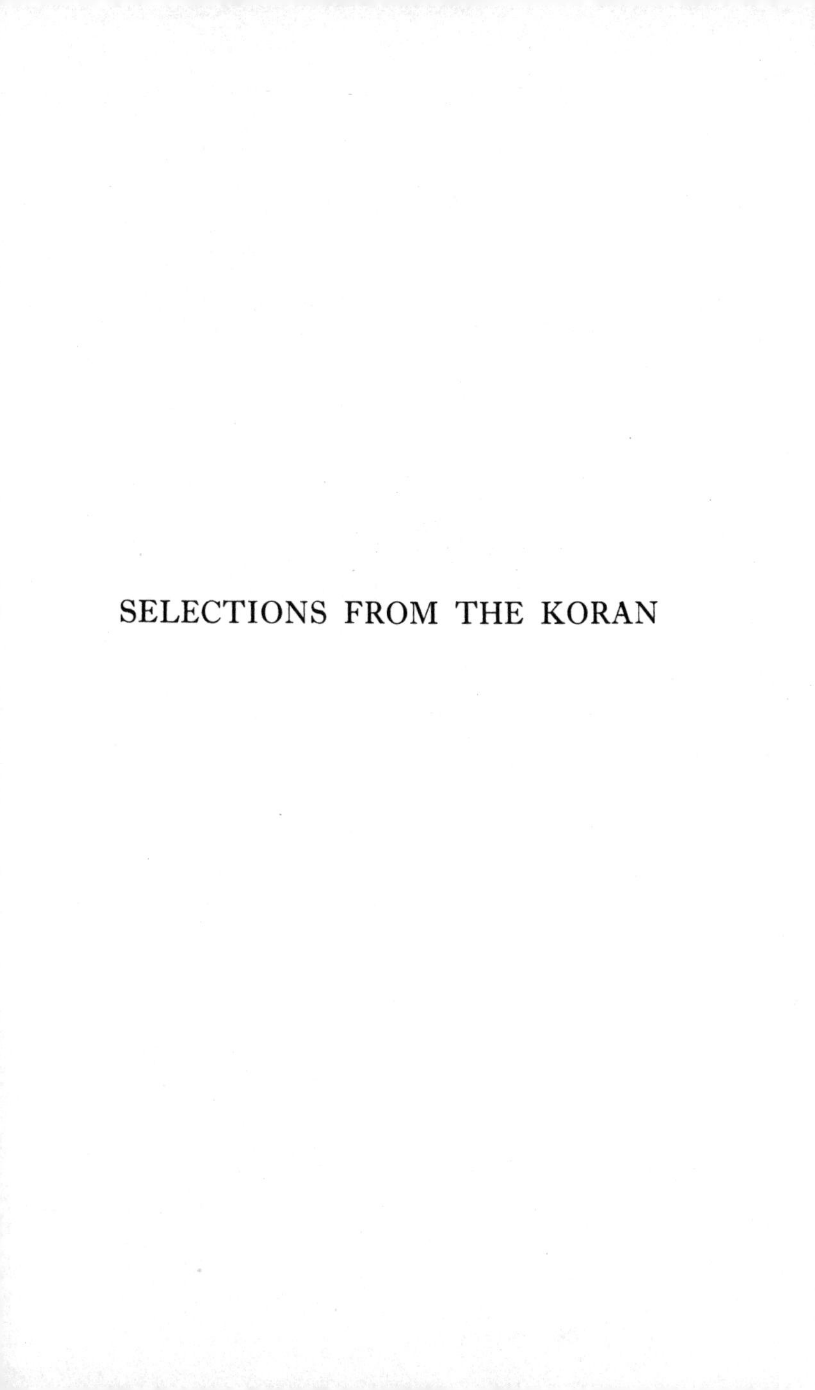

SELECTIONS FROM THE KORAN

SELECTIONS FROM THE KORAN

BY

SIRDAR IKBAL ALI SHAH

THE OCTAGON PRESS
LONDON

First Impression in this Edition 1980

ISBN 90086085 5

Printed and bound in Great Britain by
REDWOOD BURN LIMITED
Trowbridge & Esher

PREFACE

For the benefit of those readers who cannot peruse the Koran in Arabic in which it was originally inspired, and who are not familiar with its subject-matter and traditions, it is necessary to preface this collection of extracts from it by a brief explanatory statement.

The Koran, which is spelt by Moslem people as Al Quran, is the scriptural book of Islam, and was revealed to the Prophet Mohamed for mankind by divine authority. The language in which it is written is the purest form of Arabic known to scholarship, so just and eloquent in its idiom and quality that, although frequently challenged to produce even a few verses to equal its beauty of expression, the non-Moslem poets of the Prophet's era found themselves unequal to the task, and were compelled to admit that it impressed them as being a work more divine than human.

" The Book ", as devout Moslems call it, was not revealed at one time to the Prophet Mohamed, but at different periods throughout his prophetic career. He was inspired to receive it in the first instance on the heights of Mecca, during a night of prayer in the year A.D. 610, when he was forty years of age. On that occasion the following verse was vouchsafed to him:

" Read, in the name of your Lord, who created,
He created man from a clot,
Read, and your Lord is Most Honourable,
Who taught (to write) with pen,
Taught man what he knew not.
Nay, man is most surely inordinate."

This verse is known as " the Clot ", because of the outstanding word of the verse. From the date in question, more or less continuously for the next twenty-three years—that is until the death of the Prophet—the work of revelation proceeded, until by degrees the whole of the Koran was unveiled.

The manner of revelation was thus: When the Prophet felt himself inspired as the medium of divine utterance, he called for Zaid, his secretary, or, failing him, for some available scribe or amanuensis, to whom he dictated a number of verses, sometimes of considerable length, sometimes comparatively brief. The order in which the verses were to stand was arranged by the Prophet Mohamed himself, so that at the time of his demise the entire Koran was in complete written form. At that date its contents were widely known, and thousands of people had either read or heard it read so frequently, that they could recite it word for word without the slightest error. By this means the tenets of the Moslem faith were easily and quickly disseminated throughout the several Islamic countries, and even to-day public reading or reciting of the Koran is one of the most usual methods of spreading the faith.

Some six months after the death of the Prophet, the first Khalifa, Abu Bakr, at the behest of the second Khalifa, Omar, caused the pages of the Koran to be collected, and arranged its material into book form. The volume thus compiled came into the possession of Omar, who bequeathed it to his sister. The third Khalifa, Usman, had a number of accurate copies made from the original text for the use of the faithful throughout Arabia.

It is the proud boast of the Moslem worshipper that the book he cherishes has not been altered by a single letter or even by a diacritical point since it was reduced to writing from the utterance of the Prophet thirteen centuries ago. This is, indeed, quite the most remarkable claim of its kind in the history of sacred literature. When one recalls how the sacred books of other creeds have been altered and tampered with, until scholars have hesitated to credit them with any authority whatever, the unimpeachable authenticity of the Koran must be regarded as among the phenomena of the world's inspired revelations.

The Koran in its essence is descriptive of a code, or system of morality, ethics and life-conduct of the most comprehensive character. It lays down a rule or " way " of life for the faithful Moslem of the fullest and most meticulous kind. He believes that there is nothing outside its scope.

The Koran, according to the Moslem code, supplies sound direction for all the affairs and perplexities of life. The pious Moslem, when in doubt as to his line of conduct, searches his memory for the text appropriate to the situation, and never fails to find it. Thus, besides being an ethical guide and a handbook of morality, the Koran is also a book of good manners and an authority on the humanities.

No Moslem is permitted in any way to alter the text of the Koran, and in translating it the most extraordinary care has to be exercised. Millions of people commit it to memory every year and recite it during the month of fasting in its entirety.

It is not to be implied that the extracts from the Koran which appear in the following pages are in any way representative or embracive of the spirit of the Koran as a whole, or that they have been selected as the choicest passages of that immortal work. My selection has, indeed, been dictated almost entirely by considerations of modern utility, that is, I have tried to confine it to excerpts which seemed to me to supply guidance on the problems of modern life.

I hope, however, that the reader will not remain content with mere excerpts, but will be encouraged by their perusal to read the Koran as a whole for the sake of the nobility and beauty of its grave philosophy and its wise and courageous humanity, as well as for the emanation of the divine spirit of which it is eloquent.

The religion inculcated by the Prophet Mohamed is a purely monotheistic one, that is, it recognizes one God alone, and is, indeed, the only religion in the world which separates the identity of God from all other relationships. In so doing it makes a very clear and cogent appeal to the natural instinct in mankind to believe in one almighty Father and Creator, perfect and unparalleled. The way of life set forth in the Koran is that of virtue unalloyed. In no other religion, perhaps, is virtue so plainly shown to be its own reward.

Sin carries with it the germs of future punishment, which

cannot be avoided. To sin against the law of God as revealed in the Koran is assuredly to invite consequences of chastisement if the misdemeanour be petty, or disaster to soul and body if it be serious. Thus man makes his own fate, he is not inexorably led by destiny, as so many non-Moslem writers on the Islamic religion would have us believe, but has perfect free-will inasmuch as, although " the scheme of things entire " has been planned by the Almighty from the beginning, a large margin of absolute freedom has been left to individual conduct.

The Prophet Mohamed found the religion of his people a low form of tribal fetishism and superstition, incorporating the worship of stones and similar objects. The feeble sanction this belief retained among them was insufficient to check irregularities of the grossest kind. Immorality and dishonesty were rife among the Arabs of his youth, and the law, both religious and civil, was more honoured in the breach than in the observance.

These abuses the Prophet set himself to abolish. He recognized that under such a degrading paganism as then obtained in Arabia the race was bound to deteriorate and finally disintegrate and disappear, unless a higher form of faith were adopted. In seeking for this, he was guided by a natural instinct, to cast himself on the compassion of that unknown God who, he felt rather than knew, must govern the Universe.

After making an exhaustive study of other religions, he discovered in them some things that were of excellence, and this he freely acknowledged in a manner of such frankness as has never been equalled in the course of religious controversy. But in these systems he was repelled by the invasion of the idea of strict monotheism by tenets which in one way or another detracted from the supremacy of the personality of God, to which he adhered with an inspired insistence of faith.

Imitating the ancient patriarchs of his race, he sought to walk with God. Much of his mystical methods and philosophy is indeed due to the influence of patriarchal tradition, and in this he was surely and soundly guided, as it was in consonance with the whole ancient practice and higher thought of the Semitic peoples.

Seeking diligently for God, steeping himself in the essence of the emanation of the Absolute, he at length became conscious of his worthiness and ability to act as the medium of divine revelation. Then, the heavenly afflatus descended upon him, and he did not shrink from the public utterance of what had been revealed to him. At first his fellow-countrymen were inclined to scoff at what they believed to be his pretensions to inspiration, for in his case, as in that of others, credence for prophets in their own country is far to seek.

But eventually they could not fail to be impressed by an earnestness and a conviction so intense and so manifestly unselfish. The best elements among his people recognized that if the world is to be saved from comparative ruin it must embrace the teaching and system of this man who spoke out of divine authority, and who pointed to them the way out of shame and confusion to the path of honour and order.

In time the native goodness that is in all peoples responded to the Prophet's appeal, and gradually grew daily and burgeoned into a passionate enthusiasm for righteousness which swept the dregs of the old paganism and immorality before it into oblivion. But the Prophet Mohamed, even in the height of success, maintained a singleness of purpose which revealed the genuineness of his intention. A man of less faith or righteousness, carried away by the success of his plan, might have made pretensions to divine origin or supernatural character. But it is to the everlasting glory of the Prophet that he not only disdained and discredited all assumptions of the kind, but sternly discouraged them. That he, a human man, had been made the mouthpiece of the living God, was, he maintained, a circumstance of more value to mankind than if he had possessed any association with divinity, as it proved the ability of man, would he worthily and humbly approach the Creator, to achieve direct communication with God.

If the legal code of secular conduct laid down by the Prophet is strict, it was so dictated by the social looseness which preceded his season of authority. But this notwithstanding, it is agreed by all sound critics that it is capable of expansion and adaptation to modern uses and necessities. It contains the germ of all worldly polities and moral and behaviourist codes and systems. It is so constructed that its application to the larger issues and problems of modern existence is not only perfectly feasible, but capable of any rational extension by persons of honest purpose, and its value from this point of view has long been recognized not by the jurists and doctors of Islam alone, but by those of other faiths and codes.

My unqualified thanks are due to that great and distinguished savant and tireless worker for Islam, Fadilut Maab Hadrat Molvi Mohamed Ali, from whose translation of the Koran, and by whose kind permission, I make these Extracts. To facilitate reference to the complete translation, the chapter, section, verse and footnote numbers appearing in that work have been retained here. My thanks are also due to the encouragement and guidance of His Royal Highness Sirdar Shah Wali Khan, whose devotion to Islamic studies is widely known. Here I should like to conclude on the note supplied by a verse of the Koran.

" This day I have perfected for you your religion, and completed My favour on you, and chosen for you Islam as a religion."

ALFAQIR
SYED IQBAL.

LONDON, *10th July, 1932*

CONTENTS

THE OPENING
(AL-FATIHAH)

In the name of Allah
The Beneficent, The Merciful.

ALL PRAISE IS DUE TO ALLAH,
THE LORD OF THE WORLDS.
THE BENEFICENT, THE MERCIFUL,
MASTER OF THE DAY OF JUDGMENT.
THEE DO WE SERVE
AND THEE WE BESEECH FOR HELP.
SHOW US THE RIGHT PATH,
THE PATH OF THOSE
WHOM THOU HAST FAVOURED;
NOT (the path) OF THOSE
WHO EARN THINE ANGER,
NOR OF THOSE
WHO GO ASTRAY.

SELECTIONS FROM THE KORAN

CHAPTER II *

SECTION 1

Fundamental Principles of Islam

In the name of Allah, the Beneficent, the Merciful.

1. I am Allah, the best Knower.

2. There is no doubt in it, but that this book is a guide to the pious: that is for

3. those who believe in the unseen and establish prayer and spend out of what We have given them;[17]

4. and those who believe in that which has been revealed to *you*, and that which was revealed before *you*, and they are sure of the hereafter.†

17. " Spending out " of what one has been given, signifies here charity in its widest sense; that is, charity in thought and action. The first enjoins toleration, the second imposes a duty upon the Moslems to give Zakat—poor rates—according to certain regulations.

* i.e. of the Koran.

† This is the first place where the Koran enjoins upon the faithful to regard the original versions of the Torah and the Bible as Heavenly Books.

SECTION 3

Divine Unity

21. O menkind! serve your Lord Who created you and those before you, so that you may ward off (evil).

22. Who made the earth a resting-place for you and the *heaven a canopy*, and (Who) sends down rain from the cloud; and thereby producing fruit as food for you; therefore do not set up rivals to Allah while you know.

23. And if you are in doubt as to that which We have revealed to Our servant, then produce a chapter like it,[36] and call on your *helpers* besides Allah if you are truthful.

28. How do you deny Allah and you were dead and He gave you life? Again He will cause you to die and again bring you to life, then you shall be brought back to Him.

36. A similar challenge is contained in other verses as well; where the whole of mankind is declared to be unable to produce a book like the Koran. It is believed that the Koran is a unique production of Arabic literature; it has ever been regarded as the standard of the purity of that literature, but the chief characteristic of the Book is considered to lie in the remarkable transformation which it accomplished in the minds of the people.

Section 4

Man's Vast Capabilities

30. And when *your* Lord said to the angels, I am going to place in the *earth* one who shall rule (in it), they said: What! wilt Thou place in it such as shall make mischief in it and shed blood, and we celebrate Thy praise and extol Thy holiness? He said: Surely I know what you do not know.

31. And He gave Adam [52] knowledge of all the *things*,[53] then showed them to the angels; saying: Tell Me the names of those, if you are right.

32. They said: Glory be to Thee! we have no knowledge but that which Thou hast taught us; surely Thou art the Knowing, the Wise.

33. He said: O Adam! inform them of their names. Then when he had informed them of their names, He said: Did I not say to you that I surely know what is unseen in the heavens and the earth, and (that) I know what you manifest and what you hide?

52. Neither here nor anywhere else in the Holy Koran is it affirmed that Adam was the first man, or that there was no creation by God before Adam, nor that Adam lived or man was created, or the earth made, only six thousand years ago.

53. Imam Fakhruddin Razi, the great Moslem commentator, says in explanation of this passage: " God taught Adam the attributes of things and their descriptions and their characteristics, for the attributes of a thing are indicative of its nature." This signifies the vastness of the capabilities granted to Adam, and may even refer to the faculty of speech, which is the real source of the superiority of man to the whole of creation.

Section 8

The Israelites' Degeneration

62. Surely those who believe, and those who are Jews, and the Christians, and the Sabians, whoever believes in Allah and the last day and does good, they shall have their reward from their Lord, and there is no fear for them, nor shall they grieve.[104]

104. This verse strikes at the root of the idea of a favoured nation whose members alone may be entitled to salvation. Nor should it be forgotten that salvation cannot be attained by mere lip-profession even by the Moslems, or by any other people unless they adhere to a true belief and good actions. As to those who stick to their own religions, " Allah will judge between them on the day of resurrection ". It may, therefore, be noted that the existence of good men in other religions is not denied by the Holy Koran.

Section 11

Their Rejection of the Prophet

87. And most certainly We gave Moses the book and We sent apostles after him one after another: and We gave Jesus, the son of Mary, clear arguments and strengthened him with the holy *revelation*. What! whenever then an apostle came to you with that which your souls did not desire, you were insolent, so you called some prevaricators and some you slew.*

* These remarks are, of course, addressed both to the non-believers and to those who, whilst they had a Book, yet persecuted God's Messengers.

SECTION 13

Former Scriptures are abrogated

106. Whatever communication We abrogate or cause to be forgotten, We bring one better than it or like it. *Do you* not know that Allah has power over all things? [152]

107. *Do you* not know that Allah's is the kingdom of the heavens and the earth, and that besides Allah you have no guardian *or* helper?

152. This does not run counter to verse No. 4, in as much as the Books before the Koran were abrogated, yet it is enjoined upon the faithful to believe that these books, in their original form, were God's words and commandments: the only notable point being that their orders were replaced by the new law of the Koran, yet they have not ceased to be Heavenly Books. The law, according to this verse, is only modified to its complete and final shape in the Koran, which shall remain binding to the Day of Judgment according to the Moslem belief.

SECTION 14

Perfect Guidance is only in Islam

115. And Allah's is the East and the West, therefore whither you turn, thither is Allah's purpose; surely Allah is Magnanimous and Knowing.

116. And they say: Allah has taken to Himself a son. Glory be to Him; rather, whatever is in the heavens and the earth is His; all are obedient to Him.[161]

118. And those who have no knowledge say:

Why does not Allah speak to us or a sign come to us? [164] Even thus said those before them, the like of which they say; their hearts are all alike. Indeed We have made the communications clear for a people who are indubious.

119. Surely We have sent *you* with the truth as a bearer of good news and as a warner, and *you shall* not be called upon to answer for the companions of the flaming fire.

161. According to the Moslem belief the doctrine that God has a son is refuted here, as also the pagan Arab idea that the angels were the daughters of God. Some Jews paid a like reverence to Ezra.

To all these ideas an emphatic denial is given, because these limitations would be imposed upon the Divine Attributes if the suggestion was taken even remotely literally. Taken metaphorically, the idea gives rise to misunderstanding in as much as everything in the heavens and the earth and in creation is none other than His creature, His manifestation, but not His child in a circumscribed sense, which may connote the sharing of Divinity of God by a person or thing. In the eyes of Islam that is the greatest offence. As creatures they all equally proceed out of His hands. The doctrine of sonship is mentioned here as being opposed to the religion which requires entire submission from every man, and thus dispenses with the necessity of a conciliator.

164. The unbelievers refused to accept the truth of Islam unless either Allah spoke to them, so that they should have a proof that He sends His messages to men, or that a sign should come to them. The sign which they often demanded was the threatened punishment.

Section 16

Comprehensiveness of Religion

133. Nay! were you witnesses when death visited Jacob, when he said to his sons: What

will you serve after me? They said: We will serve your God and the God of your fathers, Abraham and Ishmael and Isaac, one God only, and to Him do we submit.

136. Say: We believe in Allah and (in) that which has been revealed to us, and (in) that which was revealed to Abraham and Ishmael and Isaac and Jacob and the tribes, and (in) that which was given to Moses and Jesus, and (in) that which was given to the prophets from their Lord; we do not make any distinction between any of them, and to Him do we submit.[175]

175. This shows the wide range of a Moslem's belief. Not only is belief in the great prophets of Israel an article of faith with a Moslem, but the words *that which was given to the prophets from their Lord* make the Moslem conception of belief in prophets of world-wide comprehensiveness.

Section 17

Mecca as the Centre

144. Indeed We see the turning of *your* face to heaven, so We shall surely turn *you* to a Qiblah which *you shall* like; turn then *your* face towards the Sacred Mosque, and wherever you are, turn your faces towards it, and those who have been given the Book most surely know, that it is the truth, from their Lord;[188] and Allah is not at all heedless of what they do.

188. It is reported that the Prophet Mohamed speaks of himself as "*the prayer of my father Abraham*". The followers of the Book, according to the Moslem belief, knew that not only had Abraham prayed for the appearance of a prophet

from among the sons of Ishmael, but that God had also promised a " blessing ". The Sacred House, Qiblah, which Abraham had purified with his own hands, at the place where he left Ishmael, must therefore have been known to the Israelites as the fount of Islam.

Section 18

Reason for making Mecca the Centre of Islam

148. And every one has a direction to which he turns (himself), therefore hasten to (do) good deeds; wherever you are, Allah will bring you all together; surely Allah has power over all things.[191]

149. And from whatsoever place *you come* forth, turn *your* face towards the sacred mosque; and surely it is the very truth from *your* Lord, and Allah is not at all heedless of what you do.

152. Therefore remember Me, I will remember you, and be thankful to Me and do not be ungrateful to Me.[194]

191. The clear inference being that Allah desired to focus the attention of all the faithful towards one ideal; and therefore required them to turn their faces to one specified direction, thus establishing the unity of thought and action. The unity of the *Qiblah* among the Moslems really stands for their *unity of purpose* as being a people who strive after one goal, and forms the basis on which rests the brotherhood of Islam; hence the saying of the Prophet: *Do not call those who follow your Qiblah unbelievers*.

It must, however, be noted that the Ka'aba (Sacred Shrine in Mecca), as a structure, has never been regarded as possessing any Divine or Supernatural attribute, nor do Moslems address prayers to it as a building; hence, it is incomprehensible how a conclusion is reached, that the honour thus given to the Ka'aba is a remnant of the pre-Islamite Arab polytheism or idolatry.

Even the idolatrous Arabs never worshipped the Ka'aba, though they placed in it idols to which they prayed. It should also be borne in mind that the famous black stone was not one of the Arab idols, nor can the kissing of it in performing the Moslem pilgrimage be regarded as a legacy of idolatry. That stone stands only as a mere symbol: "The stone which the builders refused is become the headstone of the corner" (*Ps.* 118: 22). Ishmael was looked upon as rejected, and the covenant was considered to have been made with the children of Isaac or Israelites, yet it was that rejected stone, for which the black stone at Ka'aba, the place where Ishmael was cast, stands as a monument, that was to become "the headstone of the corner". The black stone is unhewn, so it is the stone that was "cut out of the mountain without hands" (*Dan.* 2: 45). Jesus Christ made this clear in the parable of the husbandmen, when he plainly told the Israelites that the vineyard (i.e. the kingdom of God) would be taken away from them and given to "*other* husbandmen", i.e. to a non-Israelite people, immediately giving indication of that people in the words: "Did ye never read in the Scripture, The stone which the builders rejected, the same is become the head of the corner?" (*Matt.* 21: 42), and again emphasized his object in the words: "The kingdom of God shall be taken from you, and given to a nation bringing forth the fruits thereof" (*Matt.* 21: 43), thus showing that he was referring to a rejected nation. Hence if the black stone is kissed, it is not kissed as an idol or as a god, but as a symbol.

194. Man's remembrance of Allah is to walk humbly in His ways, and Allah's remembrance of man is to pour His blessings upon him. But as the word *zikr* in the Arabic text also means *eminence*, the meaning may therefore be, *therefore remember Me* or *glorify Me*; *I will make you eminent*.

Section 19

Those Slain in Allah's Way not dead

154. And do not speak of those who are slain in Allah's way as dead; nay, (they are) alive, but you do not perceive.[197]

156. Who, when a misfortune befalls them, say: Surely we are Allah's, and to Him we shall surely return.

157. Those are they on whom are blessings and mercy from their Lord, and those are the followers of the right course.

163. And your God is one God! there is no god but He; He is the Beneficent, the Merciful.[202]

197. That those who sacrifice their lives in the cause of truth never die is a truth which is generally recognized. As truth lives and falsehood must die, so those who make the triumph of truth the object of their lives do not die, even if they are slain in the cause of truth. Taken in a more literal sense, those who fall in the Holy Wars, according to Islamic belief, do not die the ordinary man's death; their examples, their deeds, and their souls survive: and their reward is great in the Hereafter. This verse more than any other verse in the Koran has strengthened the faithful in many a battle fought in the name of Islam, when often defeat has been turned into victory.

202. The introduction of the formula of Divine Unity in this, the concluding verse of the section, is to show that this was the cardinal fact set before the Moslems, while its ultimate result is more clearly set forth in another place to exhort the Moslems to bear all trials and tribulations cheerfully, in the name of Allah.

Section 21

Prohibited Foods

168. O men! eat the permissible and wholesome things out of what is in the earth, and do not follow the footsteps of the Satan; surely he is your open enemy;[207]

172. O you who believe! eat of the good things

that We have provided you with, and give thanks to Allah if Him it is that you serve.

173. He has only forbidden you what dies of itself, and blood, and flesh of swine, and that over which any other (name) than (that of) Allah has been invoked; but whoever is driven to necessity, not desiring, nor exceeding the limit, no sin shall be upon him; surely Allah is Forgiving, Merciful.

207. Amongst other commands now the subject of prohibited foods is introduced with a twofold object. In the first place it enjoins that only lawful and good things should be eaten. The lawful things are not only those which the law has not declared to be forbidden, but even unforbidden things become unlawful if they are acquired unlawfully, by theft, robbery, cheating, bribery, &c.

Secondly, by adding the injunction *do not follow the footsteps of the devil*, the real object of the prohibition is made plain: for there is not the least doubt that food plays an important part in the formation of character, because foul food begets foul body and mind, which thus handicapped would not be able to rise to the nobler purpose of life.

Section 22

Retaliation and Bequests

177. It is not righteousness that you turn your faces towards the East and the West, but righteousness is *this that one* should believe in Allah and the last day and the angels [214] and the Book [215] and the prophets, and give away wealth out of love for Him [216] to the near of kin and the orphans and the needy and the wayfarer and the beggars and for (the emancipation of) the captives, and keep up

prayer and pay the poor-rate; and the performers of their promise when they make a promise, and the patient in distress and affliction and in time of conflict—these are they who are true (to themselves), and these are they who are pious.

178. O you who believe! retaliation is prescribed for you in the matter of the slain: the free for the free, and the slave for the slave, and the female for the female,[220] but if any remission is made to any one by his (aggrieved) brother, then prosecution (for the blood-wit) should be made according to usage, and payment should be made to him in a good manner; this is an alleviation from your Lord and a mercy; so whoever exceeds the limit after this, he shall have a painful chastisement.

214. A belief in angels is spoken of as one of the basic principles of Islam. The belief in angels may not be as universal as a belief in the Divine Being, but it is accepted generally in all monotheistic religions. As in the case of all other principles of faith, Islam has pointed out a certain significance underlying the belief in angels. Just as our physical faculties are not by themselves sufficient to enable us to attain any object in the physical world without the assistance of other agents—as, for instance, the eye cannot see unless there is light—so our spiritual powers cannot by themselves lead us to do good or evil deeds, but here too intermediaries, which have an existence independent of our internal spiritual powers, are necessary to enable us to do good. Now, there are two opposing forces to which man is exposed—the attraction to good, or to rise up to the higher spheres of virtue, and the inclination to evil, or to stoop to a bestial life; but to bring these attractions into operation external agencies are needed, as they are needed in the case of the physical powers of man.

The external agency which brings the attraction to good

into work is termed an *angel*, and that which assists in the working of the attraction to evil is called the *devil*. If we respond to the forces of goodness, we are following the Divine Spark, and if we respond to the attraction for evil we are following Satan. The Islamic belief in angels carries, therefore, the inference that whenever we feel a tendency towards the doing of good we should at once obey that call, and follow the inviter to good. It should also be noted that, while a belief in angels constitutes an article of faith, the Moslems are not required to "believe" in devils, because, although their existence is as certain as is that of the angels, we are plainly told that we should "disbelieve" in them. A disbelief in the devil, therefore, means that we should repel the attraction for evil, as a belief in angels means that we should follow the inviter to good.

215. While a belief in all the prophets is stated to be necessary, *the Book* is spoken of here in the singular, though clearly the books of all the prophets are to be considered as included in the injunction. The reason seems to be that, elsewhere it is said that the Koran is a Book "wherein are all the right books", so that a belief in the Koran includes a belief in all these books.

216. The love of Allah is here, as in many other places in the Holy Koran, stated to be the true incentive to all deeds of righteousness.

220. The Hebrew law of retaliation is modified in Islam, being limited only to cases of murder, while among the Jews it extended to all cases of grievous hurt. But in Islam "retaliation is prescribed for you in the matter of the slain", which amounts to saying that the murderer shall be put to death. After promulgating that law in general terms, the Koran proceeds to describe a particular case, viz. that if a free man is the murderer, he himself is to be slain; if a slave is the murderer, that slave is to be executed; if a woman murdered a man, it was she that was to be put to death. The pre-Islamic Arabs used in certain cases to insist, when the person killed was of noble descent, upon the execution of others besides the murderer; they were not content with the execution of the slave or the woman, if one of them happened to be the murderer.

Section 23

Fasting

183. O you who believe! fasting is prescribed for you, as it was prescribed for those before you, so that you may be righteous.[225]

185. The month of Ramadán [227] is that in which the Al Quran [228] was revealed, a guidance to men and clear proofs of the guidance and the distinction; therefore whoever of you is present in the month, he shall fast therein, and whoever is sick or upon a journey, then (he shall fast) a (like) number of other days; Allah desires convenience for you, and He does not desire for you difficulty, and (He desires) that you should complete the number (of these fasts) and that you should exalt the greatness of Allah, for His having guided you, and that you may be grateful.

187. It is made lawful to you to go in to your wives on the night of the fast; they are an apparel for you and you are an apparel for them; so now be in contact with them and seek what Allah has ordained for you, and eat and drink until the whiteness of the day becomes distinct from the blackness of the night at dawn, then complete the fast till night, and have not contact with them while you keep to the mosques; these are the limits of Allah, so do not go near them. Thus does Allah make clear His communications for men that they may guard (against evil).

188. And do not appropriate your property

among yourselves by false means, *neither* seek to gain access thereby to the judges, in order to bring in your possession a part of the property of men wrongfully while you know.[235]

225. Fasting is a religious institution almost as universal as prayer, and in Islam it is one of the four fundamental practical ordinances, the other three being prayer, paying poor-rate, and performing the pilgrimage. The words of the Koran show that fasting was enjoined on all nations by the prophets who passed before the Holy Prophet Mohamed. "Fasting has in all ages, and among all nations, been an exercise much in use in times of mourning, sorrow, and afflictions." Likewise the Christians were commanded by Jesus to keep the fasts: "Moreover, when ye fast, be not as the hypocrites, of a sad countenance . . . But thou, when thou fastest, anoint thine head and wash thy face" (*Matt.* 6: 16, 17). Again, when the Pharisees objected to Jesus' disciples not keeping the fast as often as John's, his only answer was that when he will be taken away "then shall they fast in those days" (*Luke* 5: 33–35).

But Islam has introduced quite a new meaning into the institution of fasting. Before Islam, fasting meant the suffering of some privation in times of mourning and sorrow; in Islam, it becomes an institution for the improvement of the moral and spiritual condition of man. This is plainly stated in the concluding words: *So that you may guard against evil*, or *that you may be righteous*. The object being that man may learn how to subordinate the evil in him; and hence fasting in Islam does not mean simply abstaining from food, but from every kind of evil. In fact, abstention from food is only a step to make a man realize that if he can, in obedience to Divine injunctions, abstain from that which is otherwise lawful, how much more necessary it is that he should abstain from the evil ways which are forbidden by God.

227. The revelation of the Holy Koran commenced in the month of *Ramadán*, which is the ninth month of the Arabian year; hence, the month of *Ramadán* is particularly spoken of as being the month in which the Holy Koran was revealed. The root meaning of *Ramadán* is *excessiveness of heat*; the month was so called because "when they changed the names

of the months from the ancient language, they named them according to the seasons in which they fell, and this month agreed with the days of excessive heat". Some say that it is one of the names of Allah, for which, however, there is no reliable authority.

228. *Al-Qur-an* is the name by which the Koran was revealed to the Prophet, and it is by this name that it is frequently mentioned in the Divine revelation. The word is an infinitive noun from the root *qara-a*, which signifies primarily *he collected together the things*. The secondary significance of the root-word is *reading* or *reciting* a book. The name *Quran* embraces both meanings, for on the one hand it signifies *a book in which are gathered together* all the Divine Books, a distinction to which the Koran itself lays claim in 98: 3 and elsewhere; on the other it means *a book that is* or *should be read*.

235. The injunction to abstain from illegally taking other people's property is a fitting sequel to the injunction relating to fasting, for by fasting a man abstains from using what he has a legal right to; and, therefore, the spiritual value of fasting is made manifest. Also, the faithful are commanded not to interfere in the course of justice; nor endeavour to corrupt the judges.

Section 24

Fighting in Defence

190. And fight in the way of Allah with those who fight with you, and do not exceed the limits; surely Allah does not love those who exceed the limits.[238]

191. And kill them wherever you find them,[239] and drive them out from whence they drove you[240] out, and persecution[241] is severer than slaughter; and do not fight with them at the sacred mosque until they fight with you in it,[242] but if they do fight you, then slay them; such is the recompense of the unbelievers

192. But if they desist, then surely Allah is Forgiving, Merciful.[243]

193. And fight with them until there is no persecution, and religion should be only for Allah; but if they desist, then there should be no hostility except against the oppressors.

194. The sacred month for the sacred month and all sacred things are (under the law of) retaliation; whoever then acts aggressively against you, inflict injury on him according to the injury he has inflicted on you and be careful (of your duty) to Allah, and know that Allah is with those who guard (against evil).

238. Rabi' and Ibn-i-Zaid are of opinion that this verse is the earliest revelation regarding the permission to fight; but always in self-defence, and to observe limits. The point to be noted regarding this injunction *to fight in the way of Allah*, is that it is very often mentioned in connexion with the subject of pilgrimage, as here and in the third and twenty-second chapters. It is permissible to suppose, therefore, that war was permitted or ordained as a measure of self-defence, and to put a stop to religious persecution; the pilgrimage to Mecca, which is one of the four fundamental principles of Islam, being impossible so long as the holy place was in the hands of unbelievers, or those who hindered the pilgrims.

The first restriction to which *fighting in the way of Allah* is made subject is that the Moslems should fight only against those " who are fighting with you ". These words so conclusively show that the Moslem wars were measures of *self-defence* that a comment is hardly necessary. It shows, too, that the enemy had first taken up arms with the object of extirpating Islam—an historic fact—on which permission was granted for war. Observation of limits in warfare, lays it down that women, children, and old men who could not take up arms against the Moslems, were not to be molested. A similar exception was also made in favour of monks and hermits. And under the new conditions the civil population of towns and villages would be treated similarly, for only those are to be fought against who actually take part in fighting. A further point in relation to the prosecution of war is to be noted: especially in respect of the vanquished foes. This direction was the sore need of a community which had been subjected to the cruellest persecutions and the severest tortures at the hands of tyrants, who had neither a law nor any authority over them which should keep them within bounds. The Moslems would have been quite within their rights if in case of victory they had taken their revenge upon their persecutors; a measure of which the modern world is not entirely innocent. But they were warned beforehand that they should not exceed the limit of the bare necessity of the war.

These directions were faithfully followed by the Moslems: they were by no means the aggressors. In the very first important battle they were forced to fight against an army advancing upon Medina, the then centre of Islam, which was only three days' journey from that city. And in all their fighting they only killed or captured the armed enemy, and never harmed women, children, or old men, though their own women and children had been mercilessly put to death by the infidels.

It should be noted that it is this *defensive fighting* which is called *fighting in the way of Allah*. Fighting for the propagation of faith is not even once mentioned in the whole of the Koran, and is entirely the product of the inventive brains of the enemies of Islam. The hatred which Islam had for fighting is shown by the fact that the Moslems were not allowed to fight until the very existence of Islam was in danger. The excuses for which wars are undertaken in the modern world had long existed in the case of the Moslems, but such excuses were deemed insufficient.

The injunctions relating to fighting are given in this chapter in order to show their lenity as contrasted with the Israelite law. The first point of contrast is that in the Israelite law fighting was ordained to turn a people out of a land of which they had been the rightful owners for centuries: it was not the enemy that had taken up the sword first; whereas in Islam the Moslems were forbidden to fight except against those who first took up the sword. The second point of contrast lies in the treatment of the enemy. The Moslems were forbidden to go beyond the bare necessity of the war, and thus not only women, children, and old men were always safe in their fighting, but even the enemy's habitations, their gardens, fields, and property were safe. In the Jewish wars, however, men, women, and children were all put to death and cities were destroyed: and thus the wars of self-defence and wars of extermination are to be distinguished.

239. To kill the enemy wherever one finds him is nothing strange when a state of war exists, and yet the critics of Islam draw the most grotesque conclusions from these simple words. The verse, read together with the first, runs thus: *And fight with those who are fighting with you, and kill them wherever you find them.* And which nation fights to spare her enemies? A noted scholar says: "And the personal pronoun in the words *kill them* refers to those with whom fighting is enjoined in the previous verse." In fact, it cannot refer to anything else, nor to unbelievers generally, who are nowhere mentioned in the previous verses, not even in the previous section.

240. These words state the ultimate object of the Moslem wars: *And drive them out from whence they drove you out.* The persecutors had driven the Moslems out from their houses in Mecca and from the sacred mosque there, which was the Cradle of Islam. Thus the Moslems were ordered to carry on war against their persecutors so long as they were not dispossessed of that which they had taken possession of by force. These words further show that the enemy was not to be exterminated, but only to be dispossessed of what he had unlawfully taken.

241. The word *Fitnah*, which occurs in the Arabic text and is translated into English by "*persecution*", originally means *a burning with fire*, and then *affliction*, *distress*, and *hardship*, *slaughter*, *misleading* or *causing to err*, and *seduction from faith by any means*. The Koran explains its use of the word *fitnah* in another verse: "They ask you concerning the sacred month—about fighting in it. Say: 'Fighting in it is a grave matter; and hindering (men) from Allah's way and denying Him and (hindering men from) the sacred mosque and turning its people out of it is still graver with Allah, and persecution

is graver than slaughter'," where the term *fitnah* is clearly synonymous with *hindering men from Allah's way and the sacred mosque, and denying Allah and turning people out of the sacred mosque*, thus clearly indicating a situation of persecution. Ibn-i-'Umar explained the word *fitnah* when he said: "*And there were very few Moslems* (*at first*), *so a man used to be persecuted for his religion: they either murdered him or subjected him to tortures until Islam became predominant, then there was no fitnah*, i.e. *persecution*." The object is to state that all those who persecuted the Moslems were to be treated as enemies, because persecution of the weaker party led to graver consequences than fighting; and therefore made war permissible in self-defence.

242. The sacredness of the Meccan territory was not to be violated by the Moslems, despite the awful afflictions that they had to suffer.

243. Note the limitations imposed again in Islamic law. No excess in war is allowed. The faithful were to sheathe their swords if the enemy desisted from fighting. Cases, however, are on record when the unbelievers took advantage of such directions in practising deception on the Moslems: "Those with whom you make an agreement, then they break their agreement every time", is the Koranic verse chiefly relating to these incidents.

Section 25

The Pilgrimage and the Mischief-makers

197. The pilgrimage is (performed in) the well-known months; so whoever determines the performance of the pilgrimage therein, there shall be then no foul speech nor abusing nor disputing in the pilgrimage; and whatever good you do, Allah knows it; and make provision, for surely the *benefit of* provision is the guarding of oneself, and be careful (of your duty) to Me, O men of understanding.

201. And there are some among them who say: Our Lord! grant us good in this world and good in the hereafter, and save us from the chastisement of the fire! *

Section 26

Trials and Tribulations

212. The life of this world is made to seem fair to those who disbelieve, and they mock those who believe, and those who are pious shall be above them on the Day of Resurrection: and Allah gives means of subsistence bounteously to whom He pleases.

215. They ask *you* as to what they should spend. Say: Whatever wealth you spend, it is for the parents and the near of kin and the orphans and the needy and the wayfarer, and whatever good you do, Allah surely knows it.

Section 27

Miscellaneous Injunctions

219. They ask *you* about intoxicants [280] and games of chance. Say: In both of them there is a great sin and means of profit for men, and their sin is greater than their profit. And they ask *you* as to what they should spend. Say: What you can spare. Thus does Allah make clear to you the commands, that you may reflect.

* This is the shortest and the most concise formula which defines what a Moslem is expected to believe.

280. *Khamr* is the Arabic word used in the text, it means *wine* or *grape-wine*. It has a common application *to intoxicating expressed juice of any thing* or *any intoxicating thing that clouds or obscures the intellect*, . . . and the general application is the more correct, because *khamr* was forbidden when there was not in Medina any *khamr* of grapes. It will thus be seen that the word *khamr*, not only with reference to its root meaning of *covering* the intellect, but also having regard to its usage, includes all intoxicating substances, and therefore one may make a departure in translating it as *intoxicants*, and not as *wine* or *intoxicating liquors*.

The prohibition of intoxicants in connexion with the mention of war shows that Islam wanted to inspire true courage into its followers, and disliked the reckless daring which a man shows under the influence of intoxicating liquors and which has so often led to atrocities in wars. The prohibition spoken of here as regards intoxicating liquors and games of chance is made plainer still in another verse.

The change which these simple words, " their sin is greater than their profit ", brought about in Arabia will always remain a riddle to the social reformer. The constant fighting of Arab tribes, one against another, had made the habit of drink a second nature with the Arab, and wine was one of the very few objects which could furnish a topic to the mind of an Arab poet.

Intoxicating liquors were the chief feature of their feasts, and the habit of drink was not looked upon as an evil, nor had there ever been a temperance movement among them, the Jews and Christians being themselves addicted to this evil.

Human experience with regard to the habit of drink is that of all evils it is the most difficult to be uprooted. Yet but one command was sufficient to blot out all traces of it from among a whole nation, and afterwards from the whole of the country as it came over to Islam. History cannot present another instance of a more remarkable transformation of this magnitude brought about so easily yet so thoroughly.

The use of alcohol even in smaller doses as an exhilarant (apart from its medical uses, when prescribed by a physician only when there is a question of life and death of a patient) is forbidden; for the Prophet's saying is clear in this connexion: " A small quantity of any thing of which a large quantity is intoxicating is prohibited."

SECTION 28

Divorce

226. Those who swear that they will not go into their wives should wait four months; so if they go back, then Allah is surely Forgiving, Merciful.[292]

227. And if they have resolved on a divorce,[293] then Allah is surely Hearing, Knowing.

292. By going back is meant the re-establishing of conjugal relations.

293. *Taláq*, the Arabic word in the text, is an infinitive noun from *talaqat*, said of a woman, meaning *she was left free to go her way* or *became separated from her husband*, and signifies *the dissolving of the marriage tie*. The subject of divorce, which is introduced here, is dealt with in this and the following two sections, and further on in the fourth and sixty-fifth chapters. It may be noted that the words in which the subject is introduced give a warning against resorting to this measure except under exceptional circumstances. At the conclusion of the previous verse we are told that if the husband reasserts conjugal relations after temporary separation, he is forgiven, for Allah is Forgiving, Merciful. But if he is determined to divorce, then if he is guilty of an excess against the wife he will be punished, because the epithets *Hearing* and *Knowing* are only mentioned when the act is either disapproved or highly approved, i.e. when either punishment or a reward is to be given. As reward in such a case is quite out of the question, it is clear that the words contain a warning in case injustice should be done in divorcing.

Divorce is one of the institutions of Islam regarding which much misconception prevails. The chief feature of the law is that the wife can claim a divorce according to the Islamic law, in a religious court, not in the civil court: neither Moses nor Christ conferring that right on the woman.

It may also be added here that, though divorce is allowed by Islam if sufficient cause exists, yet the right is to be exercised under exceptional circumstances. And the Prophet's memorable words, *of all the things which have been permitted to men divorce is the most hated by Allah*, will always act as a strong check on any loose interpretation of the words of the Holy Koran. There are cases on record in which the Prophet actually pronounced divorce to be illegal.

Section 29

Divorce

229. Divorce may be (pronounced) twice;[298] then keep (them) in good fellowship or let (them) go with kindness;[299] and it is not lawful for you to take any part of what you have given them,[300] unless both fear that they cannot keep within the limits of Allah; then if you fear that they cannot keep within the limits of Allah, there is no blame on them for what she gives up to become free thereby.[301] These are the limits of Allah, so do not exceed them, and whoever exceeds the limits of Allah, these it is that are the unjust.

230. So if he divorces her she shall not be lawful to him afterwards until she marries another husband; then if he divorces her there is no blame on them both if they return to each other (by marriage), if they think that they can keep within the limits of Allah; and these are the limits of Allah which He makes clear for a people who know.*

298. Another command regarding divorce is that the revocable divorce of the previous verse can be pronounced only twice. In the days of ignorance a man used to divorce his

* A divorced woman cannot be remarried to her former husband, till she has been married and divorced by another husband.

wife and take her back within the prescribed time, even though he might do this many times. Islam reformed this practice by allowing a revocable divorce twice, so that the period of waiting in each of these two cases might serve as a period of temporary separation during which conjugal relations could be re-established.

299. The next point is that the husband must make his choice after the second divorce either to retain her permanently or to bring about a final separation. The object of a true marriage union is indicated in the simple words, *keep them in good fellowship*. Where the union is characterized by quarrels and dissensions instead of good fellowship, and two experiences of a temporary separation show that there is no real love in the union, and good fellowship is therefore entirely absent, the only remedy that remains is to let the woman *go with kindness*.

When an endeavour has been made, and it shows that the illuminating spark of love is not there, then the marriage union must be looked upon as a failure, and it is both in the interests of the husband and the wife, and in the interests of society itself, that such a union should be brought to a termination, so that the parties may seek a fresh union. But even in taking this final step the woman must be treated kindly.

300. The full payment of the dowry to the woman is another command relating to the Islamic law of divorce, and it serves as a very strong check upon the husband in resorting to unnecessary divorce. The immediate payment of dowry may deter the breaking of matrimonial ties.

301. The woman, too, has a right to claim divorce. The case of Jameelah, wife of Sábit bin Qais, is one that is reported in numerous reports of the highest authority. Here it was the wife who was dissatisfied with the marriage. There was not even a quarrel, as she plainly stated in her complaint to the Prophet: " I do not find any fault with him on account of his morals (i.e. his treatment) or his religion." She only hated him. And the Holy Prophet had her divorced on condition that she returned to her husband the garden which he had made over to her as her dowry. It is even said that the husband's love for the wife was as intense as her hatred for him.

If, then, a woman could claim a divorce for no reason other than the unsuitability of the match, she had certainly the right to claim one if there was ill-treatment on the part of the husband, or any other satisfactory reason; and among the Moslems it is an established right, which can be exercised where the Law of Islam is the Law of the country. Technically such a divorce is called *Khula'*.

Section 30

Remarriage of Widows

234. And (as for) those of you who *die* and leave wives behind, they should keep themselves in waiting for four months and ten days; then when they have fully attained their term, there is no blame on you for what they do, for themselves, in a lawful manner;[310] and Allah is aware of what you do.

310. A widow must not remarry till after four months and ten days from the death of her husband: this is to show the respect due to her former husband.

Section 31

Additional Provisions for Divorced Women and Widows

241. And for the divorced women (too) provision (must be made) according to usage; (this is) a duty on those who guard (against evil).[318]

318. This provision is in addition to the dowry which must be paid to them.

SECTION 34

Compulsion in Religion forbidden

256. There is no compulsion in religion; truly the right way has become clearly distinct from *error*; therefore, whoever disbelieves in the devil and believes in Allah, he indeed has laid hold on the firmest handle, *which shall not break off*, and Allah is Hearing, Knowing.*

SECTION 35

How Dead Nations are raised to Life

260. And when Abraham said, My Lord! show me how Thou givest life to the dead, He said: What! and *do you* not believe? He said: Yes, but that my heart may be at ease. He said: Then take four of the birds, then train them to follow *you*, then place on every mountain a part of them, then call them, they will come to *you* flying; and know that Allah is Mighty, Wise.[349]

349. The answer to Abraham's query as given here is a perfectly intelligible parable. If he should take four birds and tame them, they would obey his call and fly to him even from the distant mountains. If the birds, then, obey his call, because he has reared them only, not created them, would not nations submit to the call of their Divine Master and the Author of their existence? Or if the birds, being only tamed for a short time by a man who had otherwise no control over them, become so obedient to their tamer,

* This verse has been quoted in defence of Islam, for the last 1300 years, to show that the religion of the Koran did not permit conversion by force.

has not Allah the power to control all those causes which govern the life and death of nations? That whenever He wishes to destroy a people He brings together the causes of their decline and evil fortune overtakes them, and when He wishes to make a people prosperous He creates those causes that bring about the rise and progress of nations, is well said. The history of nations from the beginning of time proves the contention.

Section 36

Spending in the Cause of Truth

261. The parable of those who spend their property in the way of Allah, is as the parable of a grain growing seven ears (with) a hundred grains in every ear; and Allah multiplies for whom He pleases; and Allah is Ample-giving, Knowing.[351]

263. Kind speech and forgiveness is better than charity *followed by* injury; and Allah is Self-sufficient, Forbearing.

351. The comparison of money spent in the cause of truth to a grain yielding seven-hundredfold fruit is to show, firstly, that the progress of Islam should depend on the sacrifices which the individual members of the community make, and secondly, that the expenditure of money must be accompanied with hard labour, as a seed cast on untilled ground unaccompanied by any labour would not grow. It is noteworthy that, in a similar parable of Jesus, the promise contained is: thirty, sixty, or at the most a hundredfold increase (*Matt.* 13: 23; *Mark* 4: 8).

SECTION 37

Giving in the Way of Allah

271. If you give alms openly, it is well, and if you hide it and give it to the poor, it is better for you;[358] and this will do away with some of your evil deeds; and Allah is aware of what you do.

358. The *manifesting of charity* or *giving alms openly* is a thing quite different from giving them " to be seen of men ". By the giving of alms openly is meant the giving of subscriptions for works of public utility or for national defence, or for the advancement of the national cause or public welfare, in addition to giving to individuals.

SECTION 38

Usury Prohibited

275. Those who swallow down usury cannot arise, except as one whom the devil has prostrated by (his) touch he rises[364]. That is because they say, Trading is only like usury; and Allah has allowed trading and forbidden usury.[365] To whomsoever then the admonition has come from his Lord, then he desists, he shall have what has already passed,[366] and his affair is in the hands of Allah; and whoever returns (to it)—these are the inmates of the fire: they shall abide in it.

280. And if (the debtor) is in straitness, then let there be postponement until (he is in) ease; and that you remit (it) as alms is better for you, if you knew.[371]

364. *Ribá*: the Arabic word as used in the text here (literally, *an excess* or *addition*), signifies *an addition over and above the principal sum that is lent* and includes *usury* as well as *interest*. The subject is introduced here very appropriately, for as charity is the broad basis of human sympathy, usury annihilates all sympathetic affection and leads to the extreme of miserliness. Thus from one point of view the subject of usury stands in contrast with that of charity, while from another point of view the connexion between these two subjects is, as pointed out in the two preceding sections and the verse with which this section opens, that while the Moslems were promised great wealth and prosperity, they were warned against an inordinate desire for amassing wealth, to which usury would certainly have led them. Hence, those who devour usury are compared to those prostrated by the touch of the devil, which in this case stands for Mammon. Islam does not go the extreme of the socialistic idea which aims at the annihilation of all distinctions of property rights, but it establishes institutions which give the poor a definite proportion of the riches of the wealthier members of society. That is the institution of *Zakát*, or the poor rates, according to which one-fortieth portion of the amassed wealth of every member of society is taken yearly to be distributed among the poor.

In accordance with that institution, Islam refuses to allow the rich to grow richer by reducing the poor to still greater poverty, which is the real aim of usury. Usury, moreover, promotes habits of idleness; but its worst effect is on morals, as it causes man to be obsessed by selfishness, and this is, in fact, what is meant by " the devil prostrating a devourer of usury ".

365. The Koran draws a distinction between trading and usury. In trade the capitalist takes the risk of loss along with the hope of profit, but in lending money on usury the whole of the loss is suffered by the man who uses his labour, while the capitalist may count upon his profit even in the case of loss in the actual concern. Hence trading stands on quite a different footing from usury.

366. Here is a prohibition to receive any interest on money lent, but if any one had actually received any interest before the prohibition he was not required to pay it back.

371. This indicates the kind of sympathy Islam demands a man shall show to other men. The poor man is not to be prosecuted and thrown into prison, but payment must be postponed till the debtor is able to pay, or, better still, the whole may be remitted, if it cannot be paid at all.

Section 39

Contracts and Evidence

282. O you who believe! when you deal with each other in contracting a debt for a fixed time, then write it down; and let a scribe write it down between you with fairness; and the scribe should not refuse to write as Allah has taught him, so he should write; and let him who owes the debt dictate, and he should be careful of (his duty to) Allah, his Lord, and not curtail any thing from it; but if he who owes the debt is not of normal understanding, or weak, or (if) he is not able to dictate himself, let his guardian dictate with fairness; and call in to witness from among your men two witnesses; but if there are not two men, then one man and two women from among those whom you choose to be witnesses, so that if one of the two errs, the second of the two may remind the other; and the witnesses should not refuse when they are summoned; and be not averse to writing it (whether it is) small or large, with the time of its falling due; this is more equitable in the sight of Allah and *assures greater accuracy in* testimony, and the nearest (way) that you may not entertain doubts (afterwards), except when it is ready merchandise which you give and take among

yourselves from hand to hand, then there is no blame on you in not writing it down; and have witnesses when you barter with one another, and let no harm be done to the scribe *or* to the witness; and if you do (it), then surely it will be a transgression in you, and be careful of (your duty to) Allah, and Allah teaches you, and Allah knows all things.

283. And if you are upon a journey and you do not find a scribe, then (there may be) a security taken into possession; but if one of you trusts another, then he who is trusted should deliver his trust, and let him be careful (of his duty to) Allah, his Lord; and do not conceal testimony, and whoever conceals it, his heart is surely sinful; and Allah knows what you do.

CHAPTER III

Section 1

The Koran and the previous Revelation, and the Rule of Interpretation

3. He has revealed to you the Book (Al Quran) with truth, verifying that which is before it, and He revealed the Torah and the Gospel [383] aforetime: a guidance for the people, and He sent the Distinction. Surely that who disbelieve in the communications of Allah—they shall have a severe chastisement; and Allah is Mighty, the Lord of retribution.

383. In the whole of the previous chapter the *Tauràt* and the *Injil*, i.e. the Torah and the Gospel, are not mentioned by name, though frequently referred to, specially the former, as *that which is with you. Tauràt* is the name given to the books of Moses, or the Pentateuch, and hence its correct rendering is the Hebrew word *Torah*. The *Tauràt* does not signify the Old Testament, because the latter is the name of the whole collection of the books of the Israelite prophets, and includes the *Tauràt*, the *Zabúr*, and other books. *Torah* in the Hebrew literature signifies *the revealed will of God*. Some commentators trace the word *Tauràt* to the root *wary*, meaning *lighting*, and thus consider its literal meaning to be *light*. The word *kitab* conveys, however, a more general significance, and signifies sometimes the Old Testament and sometimes the Bible.

The word *Injil* does not signify the New Testament, as stated by some Christian writers. According to the Koran no prophet to whom any book should have been revealed, appeared among the Israelites (or among the followers of Christ) after the death of Jesus Christ, who, being the last of the Israelite prophets, was granted a revelation called the *Injil*, which stands for the Evangel or the Gospel, and signifies literally *good tidings*. The reason why Jesus' revelation was called Gospel, or *good tidings*, according to Islamic conception, is that it gave the glad news of the advent of the last of the prophets, which is variously described in Christ's metaphorical language, as the advent of the kingdom of God (*Mark* 1: 15), the coming of the Lord (*Matt*. 21: 40), the appearance of the Comforter (*John* 14: 16), or the spirit of Truth (*John* 14: 17), &c.

Not only are the *Acts*, the *Epistles*, and the *Book of Revelation* not recognized by the Koran as parts of *Injil*, or the Gospel, but it does not even recognize the Gospels according to Matthew, &c., as the *Injil* which was revealed to Jesus Christ, though the current Gospels, the Moslems hold, might contain some fragments of the original teaching.

This view of the Gospel as taken by the Koran, is now admitted to be the correct one, as all criticism points to some original of the synoptics which is now entirely lost. The Koran nowhere suggests that the original *Injil* existed at the time of the Prophet Mohamed.

Section 2

The Unity of Allah as the Clear Basis of all Religions and its Ultimate Triumph

10. Like the striving of the people of Pharaoh, and those before them; they rejected Our communications, so Allah destroyed them on account of their faults; and Allah is severe in requiting (evil).

Section 5

The Birth and Ministry of Jesus

44. When the angels said: O Mary! surely Allah gives you good news with a word from Him (of one) whose name is the Messiah, Jesus, son of Mary, worthy of regard in this world and the hereafter, and of those who are made near (to Allah):

45. And he shall speak to the people when in the cradle and when of old age, and (he shall be) one of the good ones.

46. She said: My Lord! when shall there be a son (born) to me, and man has not touched me? He said: Even so, Allah creates what He pleases; when He has decreed a matter, He only says to it, Be, and it is.

47. And He will teach him the Book and the wisdom and the Torah and the Gospel;

48. And (make him) an apostle to the children of Israel: That I have come to you with a sign from your Lord, that I determine for you out of

dust like the form of a bird, then I breathe into it and it becomes a bird with Allah's permission, and I heal the blind and the leprous, and bring the dead to life with Allah's permission, and I inform you of what you should eat and what you should store in your houses; most surely there is a sign in this for you, if you are believers.

49. And a verifier of that which is before me of the Torah, and that I may allow you part of that which has been forbidden you,[432] and I have come to you with a sign from your Lord, therefore be careful of (your duty to) Allah and obey me.

432. The law given by Moses was upheld by all the Israelite prophets, but its deficiencies were removed and other changes introduced from time to time to make it suit the requirements of new times. These changes are particularly marked out in the teaching of Christ; the Sermon on the Mount is a sufficient proof of this statement.

Section 6

Jesus is cleared from False Charges

54. When Allah said: O Jesus! I will cause you to die and exalt you in My presence and clear you of those who disbelieve and make those who follow you above those who disbelieve to the day of resurrection; then to Me shall be your return, so I will decide between you concerning that in which you differed.

55. Then as to those who disbelieve, I will chastise them with severe chastisement in this world and the hereafter, and they shall have no helpers.

56. And as to those who believe and do good deeds, He will pay them fully their rewards; and Allah does not love the unjust.

57. This We recite to you of the communications and the wise reminder.

58. Surely the likeness of Jesus is with Allah as the likeness of Adam; He created him from dust, then said to him, Be, and he was.

Section 7

Religion of Abraham

66. Abraham was not a Jew nor a Christian, but he was (an) upright (man), a Moslem, and he was not one of the polytheists.

Section 10

The Truth of Islam, and its Testimony

95. Most surely the first house appointed for men is the one at Bekka,[467] blessed and a guidance for the nations.

96. In it are clear signs: the standing-place of Abraham, and whoever enters it shall be secure, and pilgrimage to the House is incumbent upon men for the sake of Allah,[469] (upon) every one who is able to undertake the journey to it; and whoever disbelieves, then surely Allah is Self-sufficient, above any need of the worlds.

467. Bekka is the same as Mecca, from *tabak*, meaning *the crowding together of men*. Some, however, state that it is

from a root meaning *the breaking of the neck*, and it is so named because " whenever a tyrant has forced his way to it, his neck has been broken ". Other authorities believe that Bekka is the name of the mosque, or the House itself, that is in Mecca. This is also an answer to the Jews, who objected to the Moslems making the Ka'aba, and not the Temple at Jerusalem their *Qiblah*: that is the structure towards which they may pray. They are told that the Temple at Jerusalem was erected long after Abraham, while the Holy House at Mecca was there even before Abraham, and was, in fact, the first House on earth for the worship of the Divine Being.

469. The clear signs in Mecca, as enumerated here, are three, and these, in fact, are three prophecies with regard to the future of Mecca. The first sign is that it is the standing-place of Abraham, which has already been declared to be the Moslem centre. Hence the first prophecy is that the doctrine of the Unity of the Divine Being shall be proclaimed to the whole world from this centre. The second sign is that Mecca shall always be secure, i.e. it shall not fall into the hands of an enemy who should destroy it, because, we are told, it affords security to those who enter it, which it could not do if it were not itself secure.

There is a saying of the Prophet to the effect that the Antichrist (and the plague) shall never have access to Mecca. Thus its security is assured both physically and spiritually. And the third prophecy is that a pilgrimage to the Sacred House shall continue to be made for ever, and no power in the world shall ever be able to put a stop to it.

The most striking fact about these prophecies is that they were all announced at a time when the Prophet and his followers had apparently been driven away for ever from the sacred place, when that place was in the exclusive possession of an enemy who did not allow the Moslems to visit the place, even during the sacred months; and when the small Moslem community was in danger of being wiped out by the powerful enemy.

Section 11

Moslems must remain United

102. And hold fast by the covenant of Allah all together, and be not disunited, and remember the favour of Allah on you when you were enemies, then He united your hearts so by His favour you became brethren; and you were on the brink of a pit of fire, then He saved you from it; thus does Allah make clear to you His communications that you may follow the right Path.*

Section 14

How Success can be achieved

129. O you who believe! do not devour usury, *making additions again and again*,[490] and be careful of (your duty to) Allah, that you may be successful.

490. It may be added here that borrowing money on interest is as much against the tenets of Islam as lending it on interest. The idea is as pertinent to the Moslem nations as to individuals; for throughout the history of Islam, whenever a Moslem prince has borrowed money—of course, on interest—invariably the territorial integrity of his people has suffered.

*The Unity of Divine Attributes, the unity of worship and ideas are enjoined again and again upon the faithful.

SECTION 15

Perseverance in the Way of Allah

143. And Mohamed is no more than an apostle; the apostles have already passed away before him; if then he dies or is killed, will you turn back upon your heels? And whoever turns back upon his heels, he will by no means do harm to Allah in the least; And Allah will reward the grateful.*

145. And how many a prophet has fought with whom were many worshippers of the Lord; so they did not become weak-hearted on account of what befell them in Allah's way, nor did they weaken, nor did they abase themselves; and Allah loves the patient.

SECTION 20

Ultimate Triumph of the Faithful

194. So their Lord accepted their prayer: That I will not waste the work of a worker among you, whether male or female, the one of you being from the other; they, therefore, who fled and were turned out of their homes and persecuted in My

* Over and over again the Koran emphasizes that the Prophet was no part of Divinity, so that Divine attributes may not be given to him. This was the more necessary on account of a comparison which has to be drawn between the Moslems and Christians even in that early period of Islamic teaching. That the faithful should regard the Prophet as a perfect man, and a messenger of God, bearing the latest and the last Book, was made the subject of repeated injunctions in the Koran.

way and who fought and were slain, I will most certainly cover their evil deeds, and I will most certainly make them enter gardens in which rivers flow: a reward from Allah, and with Allah is yet better reward.

199. O you who believe! be patient and *vie in endurance* and remain steadfast, and be careful of (your duty to) Allah, that you may be successful.

CHAPTER IV

Section 1

Duties of Guardians towards their Orphan Wards

3. And if you fear that you cannot act equitably towards orphans, then marry such women as seem good to you, two and three and four;[535] but if you fear that you will not do justice (between them), then (marry) only one or what your right hands possess; this is more proper, that you may not deviate from the right course.

4. And give women their dowries as a free gift, but if they of themselves be pleased to give up to you a portion of it, then eat it with enjoyment and with wholesome result.[537]

535. This passage *permits polygamy under certain circumstances: it does not enjoin it nor even permit it unconditionally.* It is to be observed that this chapter was revealed to guide the Moslems, under the conditions which followed the battle of Ohod, and the last portion of the last chapter deals with that battle.

In that battle 70 men out of 700 Moslems had been slain, and this decimation had largely decreased the number of males, who, being the breadwinners, were the natural guardians and supporters of the females. The number was likely to suffer a still greater diminution in the battles which had yet to be fought, while the number of women would be increased by the addition of prisoners of war. Thus many orphans would be left in the charge of widows, who would find it difficult to procure the necessary means of support. Hence, in the first verse of this chapter the Moslems are enjoined to respect the ties of relationship, and as they all came from a single ancestor, comprehensiveness is introduced into the idea of relationship, inasmuch as they are told that they are all in fact related to each other.

In the second verse the care of orphans is particularly enjoined. In the third verse we are told that if they could not do justice to the orphans, they might marry the widows, whose children would thus become their own children, and as the number of women was now much greater than the number of men, they were permitted to marry even two or three or four women. It would thus be clear that the permission to have more than one wife was given under the peculiar circumstances of the Moslem society then existing, and the Prophet's action in marrying widows, as well as the example of many of his companions, corroborates this statement. Marriage with orphan girls is also sanctioned in this passage, for there were the same difficulties in the case of orphan girls as in the case of widows, and the words are general.

537. It is necessary that a " dowry " should be given to every woman taken in marriage, whether she is a free woman, an orphan girl, or a prisoner of war. So every woman begins her married life as the owner of some property, and thus marriage is the means of raising her status, in many respects elevating her to a plane of equality with her husband.

Section 2

Law of Inheritance

11. Allah enjoins you concerning your children: the male shall have the equal of the portion of two females; then if they are more than two females, they shall have two-thirds of what the deceased has left, and if there is one, she shall have the half; and as for his parents, each of them shall have the sixth of what he has left if he has a child, but if he has no child and (only) his two parents inherit him, then his mother shall have the third; but if he has brothers, then his mother shall have the sixth after (the payment of) a bequest he may have bequeathed or a debt; your parents and your children, you know not which of them is the nearer to you in usefulness; this is an ordinance from Allah: surely Allah is Knowing, Wise.

12. And you shall have half of what your wives leave if they have no child, but if they have a child, then you shall have a fourth of what they leave after (payment of) any bequest they may have bequeathed or a debt; and they shall have the fourth of what you leave if you have no child, but if you have a child then they shall have the eighth of what you leave after (payment of) a bequest you may have bequeathed or a debt; and if a man or a woman leaves property to be inherited by neither parents nor offspring, and he (or she) has a brother or a sister, then each of

these two shall have the sixth, but if they are more than that, they shall be sharers in the third after (payment of) any bequest that may have been bequeathed or a debt that does not harm (others); this is an ordinance from Allah: and Allah is Knowing, Forbearing.

SECTION 3

Treatment of Women

19. O you who believe! it is not lawful for you that you should *take women as heritage* against (their) will; and do not straiten them in order that you may take part of what you have given them, unless they are guilty of manifest indecency, and treat them kindly; then if you hate them, it may be that you dislike a thing while Allah has placed abundant good in it.

SECTION 4

What Women may be taken in Marriage

23. Forbidden to you are your mothers and your daughters and your sisters and your paternal aunts and your maternal aunts and brothers' daughters and sisters' daughters and your mothers that have suckled you and your foster-sisters and mothers of your wives and your stepdaughters who are in your guardianship, (born) of your wives to whom you have gone in; but if you have not gone in to them, there is no blame on you

(in marrying them), and the wives of your sons who are of your own loins, and that you should have two sisters together, except what has already passed; surely Allah is Forgiving, Merciful.

SECTION 5

Women's Rights over their Earnings

32. And do not covet that by which Allah has made some of you excel others; men shall have the benefit of what they earn and women shall have the benefit of what they earn; and ask Allah of His grace; surely Allah knows all things.

SECTION 6

Disagreement between Husband and Wife

35. And if you fear a breach between the two, then appoint a judge from his people and a judge from her people; if they both desire agreement, Allah will effect harmony between them; surely Allah is Knowing, Aware.[573]

573. There is much food for reflection in this for those who think that Islam allows divorce on the slightest pretext. When a breach occurs, the Qazi's first duty is to appoint judges on both sides with the object of effecting a reconciliation; it is only when judges fail to bring about a reconciliation that a divorce is allowed. The wife can obtain a divorce through the Qazi or the judge who is legally entitled to pronounce a divorce.

SECTION 13

When and to what Extent a Murderer is Excusable

92. And it does not behove a believer to kill a believer except by mistake, and whoever kills a believer by mistake, he should free a believing slave, and blood-money should be paid to his people unless they remit it as alms; but if he be from a tribe hostile to you and he is a believer, the freeing of a believing slave (suffices), and if he is from a tribe between whom and you there is a covenant, the blood-money should be paid to his people along with the freeing of a believing slave; but he who cannot find (a slave) should fast for two months successively: a penance from Allah, and Allah is Knowing, Wise.[613]

613. A person belonging to a tribe with whom the Moslems are on terms of peace is to be treated as if he were a believer.

SECTION 15

Prayer when fighting

102. And when you are among them and keep up the prayer for them, let a party of them stand up with you, and let them take their arms; then when they have prostrated themselves let them go to your rear, and let another party who have not prayed come forward and pray with you, and let them take their precautions and their arms; (for) those who disbelieve desire that you may be

careless of your arms and your luggage, so that they may then turn upon you with a sudden united attack; and there is no blame on you, if you are annoyed with rain or if you are sick, that you lay down your arms, and take your precautions; surely Allah has prepared a disgraceful chastisement for the unbelievers.

Section 24

The Moslem Law of Inheritance

177. They ask you for a decision of the law. Say: Allah gives you a decision concerning the person who has neither parents nor offspring; if a man dies (and) he has no son and he has a sister, she shall have half of what he leaves, and he shall be her heir if she has no son; but if there be two (sisters), they shall have two-thirds of what he leaves; and if there are brethren, men and women, then the male shall have the like of the portion of two females; Allah makes clear to you, lest you err; and Allah knows all things.

CHAPTER V

Section 1

General Obligations

2. O you who believe! do not violate the signs appointed by Allah, nor the sacred month, nor

(interfere with) the offerings, nor the victims with garlands, nor those repairing to the sacred house seeking the grace and pleasure of their Lord; and when you are free from the obligations of the pilgrimage, then hunt, and let not hatred of a people—because they hindered you from the sacred mosque—incite you to exceed the limits, and help one another in goodness and piety, and do not help one another in sin and aggression; and be careful of (your duty to) Allah: surely Allah is severe in requiting (evil).

3. Forbidden to you is that which dies of itself, and blood, and flesh of swine, and that on which any other name than that of Allah has been invoked, and the strangled (animal) and that beaten to death, and that killed by a fall and that killed by being smitten with the horn, and that which wild beasts have eaten, except what you slaughter, and what is sacrificed on stones set up (for idols) and that you divide by the arrows; that is a transgression.

5. This day (all) the good things are allowed to you, and the food of those who have been given the Book is lawful for you and your food is lawful for them; and the chaste from among the believing women and the chaste from among those who have been given the Book before you (are lawful for you), when you have given them their dowries, taking (them) in marriage, not fornicating nor taking them for paramours in secret; and whoever denies faith, his work indeed is of no account, and in the hereafter he shall be one of the losers.

Section 6

Punishment of Offenders (theft)

38. And (as for) the man who steals and the woman who steals, cut off their hands as a punishment for what they have earned, an exemplary punishment from Allah; and Allah is Mighty, Wise.[693]

39. But whoever repents after his iniquity and reforms (himself), then surely Allah will turn to him (mercifully); surely Allah is Forgiving, Merciful.

693. The crime of theft, like that of fornication, is one which Islam has dealt with severely, and the punishment, which requires the cutting off of the hand of the thief, must no doubt have a deterrent effect. But as imprisonment has also been mentioned in connexion with certain cases of robbery, the ordinary crime of theft may be punished similarly, while the cutting off of a hand may be reserved as a punishment for serious cases by habitual offenders upon whom imprisonment has no deterrent effect.

The considerations which entitle the judge to make this distinction are as follows: (*a*) The punishment is called exemplary, and exemplary punishment cannot be inflicted where the crime does not demand it, or when the offender is not a habitual criminal. (*b*) The punishment is not to be inflicted if the offender repents and turns from his evil course. The next verse shows that the punishment of cutting off the hand is only for a criminal *who does not reform*, i.e. *for the habitual offender*.

What really is required is *repentance and reform*, but no one can affirm that when an offender repents he will also reform. To give him a chance to reform it is necessary that he should be given freedom of action before the more serious punishment is inflicted. (*c*) The punishment of the cutting off of hands has been mentioned in connexion with the more serious crimes spoken of in verse 33, while even those serious crimes may be punished only with imprisonment, and therefore mere stealing, which is by no means a serious offence unless it becomes habitual, need not be punished with such extreme severity. (*d*) Various incidents are related in the early history of Islam in which theft was not punished by the cutting off of hands. (*e*) Even the jurists who deduced from this verse such condign punishment for theft have been compelled to introduce many limitations, without which the verse could have no practical application; the limitation which seeks to restrict the punishment to the habitual offender is at least as reasonable as any other: indeed, even when this punishment is to be inflicted on a habitual offender, it is in that rare class known as exemplary, both to himself and others so that it may have a deterrent effect. In some European countries, the deterrent effect is in view when a death penalty is inflicted, because the psychological effect of hanging—its mere loathsomeness—serves as a deterrent upon the people's minds.

SECTION 14

Making of a Will

106. O you who believe! call to witness between you when death draws nigh to one of you, at the time of making the will, two just persons from among you, or two others from among others than you, if you are travelling in the land and the calamity of death befalls you; the two (witnesses) you should detain after the prayer (from the mosque); then if you doubt (them), they shall both swear by Allah (saying): We will not take for it a price, though there be a relative, and we will not hide the testimony of Allah, for then certainly we should be among the sinners.*

* It is one more example of the knitting together of the Moslem Society, as it shows that everywhere—at home or abroad—one Moslem has ties of brotherhood with another.

Section 16

Denial of Christ's Divinity

116. And when Allah will say: O Jesus, son of Mary! *did you* say to men, Take me and my mother for two gods besides Allah, he will say: Glory be to Thee, it did not befit me that I should say what I had no right to (say); if I had said it, Thou wouldst indeed have known it; Thou knowest what is in my mind, and I do not know what is in Thy mind; surely Thou art the great Knower of the unseen things.

117. I did not say to them aught save what Thou didst enjoin me with: That serve Allah, my Lord and your Lord; and I was a witness of them so long as I was among them, but when Thou didst cause me to die, Thou wert the watcher over them, and Thou art witness of all things;

118. If Thou shouldst chastise them, then surely they are Thy servants; and if Thou shouldst forgive them, then surely Thou art the Mighty, the Wise.*

CHAPTER VI

Section 13

Gradual Progress

102. Wonderful Originator of the heavens and the earth! How could He have a son when He

* This is one of the Commandments in virtue of which the Moslems deny the Divinity of Christ.

has no consort, and He (Himself) created every thing and He is the Knower of all things!

103. That is Allah, your Lord, there is no god but He; the Creator of all things, therefore serve Him, and He has charge of all things.

Section 19

Guiding Rules of Life

152. Say: Come! I will recite what your Lord has forbidden to you—(remember) that you do not associate anything with Him and show kindness to your parents, and do not slay your children for (fear of) poverty—We provide for you and for them—and do not draw nigh to indecencies, those of them which are apparent and those which are concealed, and do not kill the soul which Allah has forbidden except for the requirements of justice; this He has enjoined you with that you may understand.

153. And do not approach the property of the orphan except in the best manner until he attains his maturity; and give full measure and weight with justice—We do not impose on any soul a duty except to the extent of its ability; and when you speak, then be just though it be (against) a relative, and fulfil Allah's covenant; this He has enjoined you with that you may be mindful.

CHAPTER VII

Section 7

The Righteous shall Prosper

54. Surely your Lord is Allah, who created the heavens and the earth in six periods of time, and He is firm in *power*; He throws the veil of night over the day, which it pursues incessantly; and (He created) the sun and the moon and the stars, made subservient by His command; surely His is the creation and the command; blessed is Allah, the Lord of the worlds.

CHAPTER X

Section 11

The Power of God

107. And if Allah should afflict *you* with harm, then there is none to remove it but He; and if He intends good to *you* there is none to repel His grace; He brings it to whom He pleases of His servants; and He is the Forgiving, the Merciful.

CHAPTER XVI

SECTION 13

Revelation enjoins Good

90. Surely Allah enjoins the doing of justice and the doing of good (to others) and the giving to the kindred, and He forbids indecency and evil and rebellion; He admonishes you that you may be mindful.

91. And fulfil the covenant of Allah when you have made a covenant, and do not break the oaths after making them fast, and you have indeed made Allah a surety for you; surely Allah knows what you do.

96. What is with you passes away and what is with Allah is enduring; and We will most certainly give to those who are patient their reward for the best of what they did.

CHAPTER XVII

SECTION 2

Every Deed has a Consequence

11. And man prays for evil as he ought to pray for good, and man is ever hasty.

12. And We have made the night and the day two signs, then We have made the sign of the

night to pass away and We have made the sign of the day manifest, so that you may seek grace from your Lord, and that you might know the numbering of years and the reckoning; and We have explained every thing with clarity.

13. And We have made every man's actions to cling to his neck, and We will bring forth to him on the resurrection day a book which he will find wide open:

14. Read *your* book; *your* own self is sufficient as a reckoner against *you* this day.

15. Whoever goes aright, for his own soul does he go aright; and whoever goes astray, to its detriment only does he go astray; nor can the bearer of a burden bear the burden of another, nor do we chastise until We raise an apostle.*

16. And when We wish to destroy a town, We send Our commandment [1420] to the people of it who lead easy lives, but they transgress therein; thus the word proves true against it, so We destroy it with utter destruction.

1420. The meaning of these words is often misunderstood. Allah does not command people to transgress, for it is plainly stated in 7: 28, "Allah does not enjoin indecency", and again in 16: 90, "He forbids indecency and evil and rebellion". The meaning is clear: Allah sends them commandments to do good, pointing out the right path through His prophets, but as they are accustomed to lead easy lives, they transgress those commandments, and are therefore punished, because they did not follow God's path but that of the devil.

* This verse lays down quite clearly that everyone will be judged according to his actions; and by inference challenges the idea of one being answerable for the sins of another.

SECTION 3

Moral Precepts

23. And *your* Lord has commanded that you shall not serve (any) but Him and show kindness to your parents. If either or both of them reach old age, say not to them (so much as) " Ugh " nor chide them, and speak to them a kindly word.

24. And make yourself submissively gentle to them with compassion, and say: O my Lord! have compassion on them, as they brought me up (when I was) little.

26. And give to the near of kin his due and (to) the needy and the wayfarer, and do not spend wastefully.

27. Surely the squanderers are the fellows of the devils, and the devil is ever ungrateful to his Lord.

28. And if *you* turn away from them (the needy) to seek mercy from *your* Lord which *you hope* for, speak to them a gentle word.[1423]

29. And do not make *your* hand to be shackled to *your* neck nor stretch it forth to the utmost (limit) of its stretching forth, lest *you should* (afterwards) sit down blamed, stripped off.[1424]

1423. The *hoping for mercy from the Lord* means standing in need of the bounty of the Lord, i.e. *not having anything to give to the needy*. In that case one should still speak to him gently and not chide him with harshness, so that if the difficulty cannot be relieved, one's behaviour should at least be kind. A saying of the Holy Prophet declares a gentle word spoken to a fellow-man to be a deed of charity.

1424. By *the shackling of the hand to the neck* is meant *being niggardly* in one's expenses, and by *stretching it forth* to its utmost extent, *being so profuse as to waste away all one's substance*. The verse supplies a general rule regarding the mean to be adopted in one's ordinary expenses, and thus inculcates the duty of economy.

SECTION 4

Moral Precepts

31. And do not kill your children for fear of poverty; We give them sustenance and yourselves (too); surely to kill them is a great wrong.[1425]

33. And do not kill any one whom Allah has forbidden except for a just cause, and whoever is slain unjustly, We have indeed given to his heir authority, so let him not exceed the just limits in slaying; surely he is aided.[1427]

34. And draw not near to the property of the orphan except in a goodly way till he attains his maturity and fulfil the promise; surely (every) promise shall be questioned about.

35. And give full measure when you measure out, and weigh with a true balance; this is fair and better in the end.

36. And follow not that of which *you have* not the knowledge; surely the hearing and the sight and the heart, all of these, shall be questioned about that.

37. And do not go about in the land exultingly, for *you can* not cut through the earth nor reach the mountains in height.*

* Much of the social wrongs would disappear if even the so-called civilized people would act on these verses; for pride and self-praise are the most prevalent vices of modern society.

1425. Infanticide, in the case of daughters, was a practice among the Arabs, because the females could not go out to war and thus procure for themselves, by means of plunder, their means of subsistence. This practice was prohibited.

1427. The words *he is aided* probably indicate that as the government is bound to aid him by bringing the murderer within reach of the law, the heir should not take the law into his own hands, but seek justice from the State.

Section 7

The Devil's Opposition to the Righteous

61. And when We said to the angels: Make obeisance, but Iblis (did it not). He said: Shall I make obeisance to him whom Thou hast created of dust?

62. He said: Tell me, is this he whom Thou hast honoured above me? If Thou shouldst respite me to the day of resurrection, I will most certainly cause his progeny to perish except a few.

63. He said: Be gone! for whoever of them will follow *you*, then surely hell is your recompense, a full recompense:

64. And beguile whomsoever of them *you can* with *your* voice, and collect against them *your* forces riding and on foot, and share with them in wealth and children, and hold out promises to them; and the devil makes not promises to them but to deceive:

65. Surely (as for) My servants, *you have* no authority over them; and *your* Lord is sufficient as a Protector.

66. Your Lord is He who speeds the ships for

you in the sea that you may seek of His grace; surely He is ever Merciful to you.

67. And when distress afflicts you in the sea, away go those whom you call on except Him; but when He brings you safe to the land, you turn aside; and man is ever ungrateful.

Section 9

Falsehood shall vanish before Truth

78. Keep up prayer from the declining of the sun till the darkness of the night and the morning recitation; surely the morning recitation is witnessed.[1457]

79. And during a part of the night, forsake sleep by it, beyond what is incumbent on *you*; maybe *your* Lord will raise *you* to a position of great glory.

80. And say: My Lord! make me to enter a goodly entering, and cause me to go forth a goodly going forth, and grant me from near Thee a power to assist (me).

81. And say: The truth has come and the falsehood vanished; surely falsehood is a vanishing (thing).

82. And We reveal of the Al Quran that which is a healing and a mercy to the believers, and it adds only to the perdition of the unjust.

83. And when We bestow favour on man, he turns aside and behaves proudly, and when evil afflicts him, he is despairing.

84. Say: Every one acts according to his manner; but your Lord best knows who is best guided in the path.

1457. From the declining of the sun to sunset are two prayers, i.e. the *zuhr* and *'asr*, or the afternoon and later afternoon prayers, while from sunset till darkness there are two others, i.e. the *maghrib* and the *'isha*, or the sunset prayer and the prayer of nightfall, and the fifth is the morning prayer, which is called here the *Qur-án-ul-fajr*, or *the morning Koran* or *morning recitation*. Thus this verse mentions all the five prayers of the twenty-four hours enjoined upon the faithful.

Section 10

The Koran is a Wondrous Miracle

85. And they ask *you* about the *revelation*. Say:
The *revelation* is by the commandment of my
Lord, and you are not given aught of knowledge
but a little.
86. And if We please, We should certainly take
away that which We have revealed to *you*, then
you would not find for it any protector against Us.
87. But on account of mercy from *your* Lord—
surely His grace to *you* is abundant.
88. Say: If men and jinn should combine
together to bring the like of this Koran, they
could not bring the like of it, though some of
them were aiders of others.
89. And certainly We have made distinct for
men in this Koran every kind of description, but
most men do not consent to aught but denying.
90. And they say: We will by no means believe

in *you* until *you* cause a fountain to gush forth from the earth for us:

91. Or *you should* have a garden of palms and grapes in the midst of which *you should* cause rivers to flow forth, gushing out:

92. Or *you should* cause the heaven to come down upon us in pieces as *you think*, or bring Allah and the angels face to face (with us):

93. Or *you should* have a house of gold, or *you should* ascend into heaven, and we will not believe in *your* ascending until *you* bring down to us a book which we may read. Say: Glory be to my Lord; am I aught but a mortal apostle?

CHAPTER XVIII

Section 9

Moses' Travels in search of Knowledge

60. And when Moses said to his servant: I will not cease until I reach the junction of the two rivers or I will go on for years;

61. So when they had reached the junction of the two (rivers), they forgot their fish, and it took its way into the sea, going away.

63. He said: *Did you* see when we took refuge on the rock, then I forgot the fish, and nothing made me forget to speak of it but the devil, and it took its way into the river; what a wonder!

65. Then they found one from among Our

servants, whom We had granted mercy from Us, and whom We had taught knowledge from Ourselves.

66. Moses said to him: Shall I follow *you* on condition that *you should* teach me right knowledge of what *you have* been taught?

67. He said: Surely *you* can not have patience with me:

68. And how *can you* have patience in that of which *you have* not got a comprehensive knowledge?

69. He said: If Allah please, *you will* find me patient and I shall not disobey *you* in any way.

70. He said: If *you would* follow me, then do not question me about any thing until I myself speak to *you* about it.

Section 10

Moses' Travels in search of Knowledge

71. So they went (their way) until when they embarked in the boat he made a hole in it. (Moses) said: *Have you* made a hole in it to drown its inmates? certainly *you have* done a grievous thing.

72. He said: Did I not say that *you will* not be able to have patience with me?

73. He said: Blame me not for what I forgot, and do not constrain me to a difficult thing in my affair.

74. So they went on until, when they met a boy, he slew him. (Moses) said: *Have you* slain

an innocent person otherwise than for manslaughter? certainly *you have* done an evil thing.

75. He said: Did I not say to *you* that *you will* not be able to have patience with me?

76. He said: If I ask *you* about any thing after this, keep me not in *your* company; indeed *you shall* have (then) found an excuse in my case.

77. So they went on until when they came to the people of a town, they asked *them* for food, but they refused to entertain them as guests. Then they found in it a wall which *was on the point of* falling, so he put it into a right state. (Moses) said: If *you had* pleased, *you might* certainly have taken a recompense for it.

78. He said: This shall be separation between me and *you*; now I will inform *you* of the significance of that with which *you could* not have patience.

79. As for the boat, it belonged to (some) poor men, who worked on the river, and I wished that I should damage it, and there was behind them a king who seized every boat by force.

80. And as for the boy, his parents were believers and we feared lest he should make disobedience and ingratitude to come upon them;

81. So we desired that their Lord might give them in his place one better than him in purity, and nearer to having compassion.

82. And as for the wall, it belonged to two orphan boys in the city, and there was beneath it a treasure belonging to them, and their father was a righteous man; so *your* Lord desired that

they should attain their maturity and take out their treasure, a mercy from *your* Lord, and I did not do it of my own accord. This is the significance of that with which you could not have patience.

CHAPTER XIX

SECTION 2

Mary and Jesus

16. And mention Mary in the Book when she drew aside from her family to an eastern place;

17. So she took a veil (to screen herself) from them; then We sent to her Our *inspiration*, and *there* appeared to her *a* well-made man.

18. She said: Surely I fly for refuge from *you* to the Beneficent God, if *you are* one guarding (against evil).

19. He said: I am only a messenger of *your* Lord: That I will give you a pure boy.

20. She said: When shall I have a boy and no mortal has yet touched me, nor have I been unchaste?

21. He said: Even so; *your* Lord says: It is easy to Me; and that We may make him a sign to men and a mercy from Us; and it is a matter which has been decreed.

22. So she conceived him; then withdrew herself with him to a remote place.

23. And the throes (of child-birth) compelled

her to betake herself to the trunk of a palm-tree. She said: Oh, would that I had died before this, and had been a thing quite forgotten!

24. Then (a voice) called out to her from beneath her: Grieve not, surely *your* Lord has made a stream to flow beneath *you*:

25. And shake towards *you* the trunk of the palm-tree, it will drop on *you* fresh ripe dates:

26. So eat and drink and refresh the eye. Then if *you see* any mortal, say: Surely I have vowed a fast to the Beneficent God, so I shall not speak to any man to-day.

27. And she came to her people with him, carrying him (with her). They said: O Mary! surely *you have done a strange thing*.

28. O sister of Aaron! *your* father was not a bad man, nor was *your* mother an unchaste woman.

29. But she pointed to him. They said: How should we speak to one who was a child in the cradle?

30. He said: Surely I am a servant of Allah; He has given me the Book and made me a prophet.

31. And He has made me blessed wherever I may be, and He has enjoined on me prayer and poor-rate so long as I live;

32. And dutiful to my mother, and He has not made me insolent, unblessed:

33. And peace on me on the day I was born, and on the day I die, and on the day I am raised to life.

34. Such is Jesus son of Mary; (this is) the saying of truth about which they dispute.

35. It beseems not Allah that He should take to Himself a son, glory be to Him; when He has decreed a matter He only says to it " Be," and it is.

36. And surely Allah is my Lord and your Lord, therefore serve Him; this is the right path.

37. But parties from among them disagreed with each other, so woe to those who disbelieve, because of presence on a great day.

SECTION 6

False Doctrine of Sonship

88. And they say: The Beneficent God has taken (to Himself) a son.

90. The heavens may almost be rent thereat, and the earth cleave asunder, and the mountains fall down in pieces,

91. That they ascribe a son to the Beneficent God.

92. And it is not worthy of the Beneficent God that He should take (to Himself) a son.

CHAPTER XX

SECTION 1

The History of Moses

9. And has the story of Moses come to *you*?

10. When he saw fire, he said to his family:

Stop, for surely I see a fire, haply I may bring to you therefrom a live coal or find a guidance at the fire.

11. So when he came to it, a voice was uttered: O Moses:

12. Surely I am *your* Lord, therefore discard *your* shoes, surely *you are* in the sacred valley, *twice*,

13. And I have chosen *you*, so listen to what is revealed:

14. Surely I am Allah, there is no god but I, therefore serve Me and worship in My remembrance:

15. Surely the hour is coming—I am about to make it manifest—so that every soul may be rewarded as it strives:

16. Therefore let not him who believes not in it, and follows his low desires, turn *you* away from it, so that *you should* perish:

17. And what is this in *your* right hand, O Moses?

18. He said: This is my staff: I recline on it and I beat the leaves with it to make them fall upon my sheep, and I have other uses for it.

19. He said: Cast it down, O Moses!

20. So he cast it down, and lo! it was a serpent running.

21. He said: Take hold of it and fear not; We will restore it to its former state:

22. And press *your* hand to *your* side, it shall come out white without evil: another sign:

23. That We may show *you* of Our greater signs:

24. Go to Pharaoh, surely he has exceeded all limits.

Section 2

The History of Moses

25. He said: O my Lord! expand my breast for me:
26. And make my affair easy to me:
27. And loose the knot from my tongue:
28. (That) they may understand my word:
29. And give to me an aider from my family:
30. Aaron, my brother:
31. Strengthen my back by him:
32. And associate him (with me) in my affair.
33. So that we should glorify Thee much:
34. And remember Thee oft:
35. Surely, Thou art seeing us.
36. He said: *You are* indeed granted *your* petition, O Moses:
37. And certainly We bestowed on *you* a favour at another time:
38. When We revealed to *your* mother what was revealed:
39. *Saying*: Put him into a chest, then cast it down into the river, then the river shall throw him on the shore; there shall take him up one who is an enemy to Me and enemy to him; and I cast down upon *you* love from Me, and that *you might* be brought up before My eyes:
40. When *your* sister went and said: Shall I direct you to one who will take charge of him?

So We brought *you* back to *your* mother, that her eye might be consoled and she should not grieve; and *you killed* a man, then We delivered *you* from the grief, and We tried *you* with (a severe) trying. Then *you stayed* for years among the people of Midian; then *you came* hither as ordained, O Moses:

41. And I have chosen *you* for Myself:

42. Go *you* and *your* brother with My communications and be not remiss in remembering Me:

43. Go both to Pharaoh, surely he has become inordinate:

44. Then speak to him a gentle word, haply he may mind or fear.

45. Both said: O our Lord! surely we fear that he may hasten to do evil to us, or that he may become inordinate.

46. He said: Fear not, surely I am with you both: I do hear and see:

47. So go you both to him and say: Surely we are two apostles of *your* Lord; therefore send the children of Israel with us, and do not torment them! Indeed we have brought to *you* a communication from *your* Lord, and peace is on him who follows the guidance:

48. Surely it has been revealed to us that the chastisement will surely come upon him who rejects and turns back.

49. (Pharaoh) said: And who is your Lord, O Moses?

50. He said: Our Lord is He Who gave to

everything its creation, then guided it (to its goal).

51. He said: Then what is the state of the former generations?

52. He said: The knowledge thereof is with my Lord in a book: my Lord errs not, nor does He forget:

53. Who made the earth for you an expanse and made for you therein paths and sent down water from the cloud; then thereby We have brought forth many species of various herbs:

54. Eat and pasture your cattle: most surely there are signs in this for those endowed with understanding.

Section 3

The History of Moses

57. Said he: *Have you* come to us that *you should* turn us out of our land by *your* enchantment, O Moses?

58. So we too will produce before you enchantment like it, therefore make between us and *you* an appointment, which we should not break, (neither) we nor *you*, (in) a central place.

59. (Moses) said: Your appointment is the day of the Festival, and let the people be gathered together in the early forenoon.

60. So Pharaoh turned his back and settled his plan, then came.

61. Moses said to them: Woe to you! do not forge a lie against Allah, lest He destroy you by a

chastisement, and he who forges (a lie) indeed fails to attain (his desire).

62. So they disputed with one another about their affair, and kept the discourse secret.

63. They said: These are most surely two enchanters who wish to turn you out from your land by their enchantment, and to take away your most *exemplary usage*.

64. Therefore settle your plan, then come standing in ranks, and he will prosper indeed this day who overcomes.

65. They said: O Moses! *will you* cast, or shall we be the first who cast down?

66. He said: Nay! cast down. Then lo! their cords and their rods—it was imaged to him on account of their enchantment as if they were running.

67. So Moses conceived in his mind a fear.

68. We said: Fear not, surely *you shall* be the uppermost:

69. And cast down what is in *your* right hand: it shall devour what they have wrought; they have wrought only the plan of an enchanter, and the enchanter shall not be successful wheresoever he may come from.

70. And the enchanters were cast down making obeisance; they said: We believe in the Lord of Aaron and Moses.

71. (Pharaoh) said: You believe in him before I give you leave; most surely he is the chief of you who taught you enchantment, therefore I will certainly cut off your hands and your feet

on opposite sides, and I will certainly crucify you on the trunks of the palm-trees, and certainly you will come to know which of us is the more severe, and the more abiding in chastising.

72. They said: We do not prefer *you* to what has come to us of clear arguments and to Him who made us, therefore decide what *you are* going to decide; *you can* only decide about this world's life:

73. Surely we believe in our Lord that He may forgive us our sins and the enchantment to which *you compelled* us; and Allah is better and more Abiding.

Section 4

The History of Moses

77. And certainly We revealed to Moses, *saying*: Travel by night with My servants, then make for them a dry path in the sea, not fearing to be overtaken, nor being afraid.

80. O children of Israel! indeed We delivered you from your enemy, and We made a covenant with you on the blessed side of the mountain, and We sent to you the manna and the quails.

CHAPTER XXI

Section 2

Truth has always triumphed

22. If there had been in them any gods except Allah, they would both have certainly been in a state of disorder; therefore glory be to Allah, the Lord of the dominion, above what they attribute (to Him).[1620]

23. He cannot be questioned concerning what He does, and they shall be questioned.

24. Or, have they taken gods besides Him? Say: Bring your proof: this is the reminder of those with me and the reminder of those before me.[1621] Nay: most of them do not know the truth, so they turn aside.

25. And We did not send before *you* any apostle but We revealed to him that there is no god but Me, therefore serve Me.

26. And they say: The Beneficent God has taken to Himself a son;[1622] glory be to Him. Nay! they are honoured servants;[1623]

27. They do not precede Him in speech and (only) according to His commandment do they act.

1620. This is a conclusive argument against polytheism. There is order in the universe because one law pervades the whole of it, and one law clearly points to one Author and Maintainer of that law. Had there been other gods, one law could not have governed the whole of the universe, and disorder and confusion would certainly have been the result. The unity of law is a clear proof of the Unity of the Maker.

1621. The great and fundamental truth of the Unity of Allah is common to all religions.

1622. This is a clear reference to the Christian doctrine of the sonship of Jesus.

1623. The meaning is, that they whom they call sons are honoured servants of Allah, the reference being to prophets, because it is a prophet whom they call a son of God. Against the doctrine that Jesus Christ is the son of God the Koran does not say that *he is an honoured servant*, but that *they are honoured servants*, which, while negativing the doctrine of the sonship of Jesus, adduces an argument against it. That argument is in the words *honoured servants*, for these words draw attention to the fact that many men were spoken of as the *sons of God*, but that the title signified nothing more than that they were honoured servants, and that therefore Jesus, according to Islamic belief, was son of God exactly in the same sense as the others.

SECTION 5

Abraham's History

51. And certainly We gave to Abraham his rectitude before, and We knew him fully well.

52. When he said to his sire and his people: What are these images to whose worship you cleave?

53. They said: We found our fathers worshipping them.

55. They said: *Have you* brought to us the truth, or *are you* one of the triflers?

56. He said: Nay! your Lord is the Lord of the heavens and the earth, Who brought them into existence, and I am of those who bear witness to this;

57. And, by Allah! I will certainly strive against your idols after you go away, turning back.

58. So he broke them into pieces, except the chief of them, that haply they may return to it.

59. They said: Who has done this to our gods? most surely he is one of the unjust.

60. They said: We heard a youth called Abraham speak of them.

61. Said they: Then bring him before the eyes of the people, perhaps they may bear witness.

62. They said: *Have you* done this to our gods, O Abraham?

63. He said: Surely (some doer) has done it; the chief of them is this, therefore ask them, if they can speak.

64. They then turned to themselves and said: Surely you yourselves are the unjust;

65. Then they were made to hang down their heads: Certainly *you know* that they do not speak.

66. He said: What! do you then serve besides Allah what brings you not any benefit at all, nor does it harm you?

67. Fie on you and on what you serve besides Allah; what! do you not then understand?

68. They said: Burn him and help your gods, if you are going to do (anything).

69. We said: O fire! be a comfort and peace to Abraham;

70. And they desired a war on him, but We made them the greatest losers.

71. And We delivered him as well as Lot, (removing them) to the land which We had blessed for all people.

72. And We gave him Isaac, and Jacob, a son's son, and We made (them) all good.

73. And We made them leaders who guided (people) by Our command, and We revealed to them the doing of good and the keeping up of prayer and the giving of the alms, and Us (alone) did they serve.

74. And (as for) Lot, We gave him wisdom and knowledge, and We delivered him from the town which wrought abominations; surely they were an evil people, transgressors;

75. And We took him into Our mercy; surely he was of the good.

CHAPTER XXII

SECTION 6

Believers permitted to Fight

39. Permission (to fight) is given to those upon whom war is made because they are oppressed, and most surely Allah is well able to assist them;

40. Those who have been expelled from their homes without a just cause (that is, because) they say: Our Lord is Allah. And had there not been Allah's repelling some people by others, certainly there would have been pulled down cloisters and churches and synagogues and mosques in which Allah's name is much remembered; and surely

Allah will help him who helps *His cause*; most surely Allah is Strong, Mighty:*

Section 10

Polytheism shall be uprooted

73. O people! a parable is set forth, therefore listen to it; surely those whom you call upon besides Allah cannot create a fly, though they should all gather for it, and should the fly carry off aught from them, they could not take it back from it; weak are the invoker and the invoked.

77. O you who believe! bow down and prostrate yourselves and serve your Lord, and do good that you may succeed.

78. And strive hard in (the way of) Allah, (such) a striving as is due to Him; He has chosen you and has not laid upon you any hardship in religion; the faith of your father Abraham; He named you Moslems before and in this, that the Apostle may be *a bearer of witness to you*, and you may be *bearers of witness* to the people; therefore worship and pay the poor-rate and hold fast by Allah; He is your Guardian; how excellent the Guardian and how excellent the Helper!

* Utmost sanctity of places of worship where unity of God is preached is enjoined upon the Moslems.

CHAPTER XXIV

SECTION 1

Law relating to Adultery

2. (As for) the fornicatress and the fornicator, flog each of them, (giving) a hundred stripes, and let not pity for them detain you in the matter of obedience to Allah, if you believe in Allah and the last day, and let a party of believers witness their chastisement.

3. The fornicator shall not marry any but a fornicatress or idolatress, and (as for) the fornicatress, none shall marry her but a fornicator or an idolater; and it is forbidden to the believers.

4. And those who accuse free women (and) then do not bring four witnesses, flog them, (giving) eighty stripes, and do not admit any evidence from them ever; and these it is that are the transgressors.

SECTION 4

Preventive Measures against Slander

27. O you who believe! do not enter houses other than your own houses until you have asked permission and saluted their inmates; this is better for you, that you may be mindful.

28. But if you do not find any one therein, then do not enter them until permission is given to you; and if it is said to you, Go back, then

go back; this is purer for you; and Allah is Cognizant of what you do.

29. It is no sin in you that you enter uninhabited houses wherein you have your necessaries; and Allah knows what you do openly and what you hide.

30. Say to the believing men that they cast down their looks and guard their private parts; that is purer for them; surely Allah is Aware of what they do.

31. And say to the believing women that they cast down their looks and guard their private parts and not display their ornaments except what appears thereof, and let them wear their head-coverings over their bosoms, and not display their ornaments except to their husbands or their fathers, or the fathers of their husbands, or their sons, or the sons of their husbands, or their brothers, or their brothers' sons, or their sisters' sons, or their women, or those whom their right hands possess, or the male servants not having need (of women), or the children who have not attained knowledge of what is hidden of women; and let them not strike their feet so that what they hide of their ornaments may be known; and turn to Allah all of you, O believers! so that you may be successful.

32. And marry those among you who are single and those who are fit among your male slaves and your female slaves; if they are needy, Allah will make them free from want out of His grace; and Allah is Amply-giving, Knowing.

33. And let those who do not find *a match* keep chaste until Allah makes them free from want out of His grace. And (as for) those who ask for a writing from among those whom your right hands possess, give them the writing if you know any good in them, and give them of the wealth of Allah which He has given you; and do not compel your slave girls to prostitution, when they desire to keep chaste, in order to seek the frail good of this world's life; and whoever compels them, then surely after their compulsion Allah is Forgiving, Merciful.

SECTION 5

Manifestation of Divine Light in Islam

39. And (as for) those who disbelieve, their deeds are like the mirage in a desert, which the thirsty man deems to be water; until when he comes to it he finds it to be naught, and there he finds Allah, so He pays back to him his reckoning in full; and Allah is quick in reckoning.

SECTION 8

Respect for each other's Privacy

58. O you who believe! let those whom your right hands possess and those of you who have not attained to puberty ask permission of you three times: before the morning prayer, and when you put off your clothes at midday in summer, and

after the prayer of the nightfall; these are three times of privacy for you; neither is it a sin for you nor for them besides these; some of you must go round about (waiting) upon others; thus does Allah make clear to you the communications, and Allah is Knowing, Wise.

59. And when the children among you have attained to puberty, let them seek permission as those before them sought permission; thus does Allah make clear to you His communications, and Allah is Knowing, Wise.

60. And (as for) women advanced in years who do not hope for a marriage, it is no sin for them if they put off their clothes without displaying their ornaments; and if they restrain themselves it is better for them; and Allah is Hearing, Knowing.

61. There is no blame on the blind man, nor is there blame on the lame, nor is there blame on the sick, nor on yourselves that you eat from your houses, or your fathers' houses, or your mothers' houses, or your brothers' houses, or your sisters' houses, or your paternal uncles' houses, or your paternal aunts' houses, or your maternal uncles' houses, or your maternal aunts' houses, or what you possess the keys of, or your friend's (house). It is no sin in you that you eat together or separately. So when you enter houses, greet your people with a salutation from Allah, blessed (and) goodly; thus does Allah make clear to you the communications, that you may understand.

SECTION 9

Matters of State should take Precedence of Private Affairs

62. Only those are believers who believe in Allah and His Apostle, and when they are with him on a momentous affair, they go not away until they have asked his permission; surely they who ask *your* permission are they who believe in Allah and His Apostle; so when they ask *your* permission for some affair of theirs, give permission to whom *you please* of them, and ask forgiveness for them from Allah; surely Allah is Forgiving, Merciful.

63. Do not hold the Apostle's calling (you) among you to be like your calling one to the other; Allah indeed knows those who steal away from among you, concealing themselves; therefore let those beware who go against his order lest a trial afflict them or there befall them a painful chastisement.

CHAPTER XXV

SECTION 1

A Warner for all Nations

1. Blessed is He Who sent down the distinction upon His servant that he may be a warner to the nations;

2. He, Whose is the kingdom of the heavens and the earth, and Who did not take to Himself a son, and Who has no associate in the kingdom, and Who created every thing, then ordained for it a measure.

Section 6

The Transformation Wrought

61. Blessed is He Who made the stars in the heavens and made therein a *sun* and a shining moon.

62. And He it is Who made the night and the day to follow each other for him who desires to be mindful or desires to be thankful.

63. And the servants of the Beneficent God are they who walk on the earth in humbleness, and when the ignorant address them, they say, Peace.

64. And they who pass the night prostrating themselves before their Lord and standing.

68. And they who do not call upon another god with Allah and do not slay the soul, which Allah has forbidden except in the requirements of justice, and (who) do not commit fornication; and he who does this shall find a requital of sin;

72. And they who do not bear witness to what is false, and when they pass by what is vain, they pass by nobly.

CHAPTER XXIX

Section 7

Triumph of the Faithful

64. And this life of the world is nothing but a sport and a play; and as for the next abode, that most surely is the life: did they but know!

69. And (as for) those who strive hard for Us, We will most certainly guide them in Our ways; and Allah is most surely with the doers of good.

CHAPTER XXX

Section 3

Manifestations of Divine Power in Nature

20. And one of His signs is that He created you from dust, then lo! you are mortals (who) scatter.

21. And one of His signs is that He created mates for you from yourselves that you may *find quiet of mind in* them, and He put between you love and compassion; most surely there are signs in this for a people who reflect.

22. And one of His signs is the creation of the heavens and the earth and the diversity of your tongues and colours; most surely there are signs in this for the learned.

23. And one of His signs is your sleeping and

your seeking of His grace by night and (by) day; most surely there are signs in this for a people who would hear.

24. And one of His signs is that He shows you the lightning for fear and for hope, and sends down water from the cloud, then gives life therewith to the earth after its death; most surely there are signs in this for a people who understand.

25. And one of His signs is that the heaven and the earth subsist by His command, then when He calls you with a (single) call from out the earth, lo! you come forth.

26. And His is whosoever is in the heavens and the earth: all are obedient to Him:

27. And He it is Who originates the creation, then reproduces it, and it is easy to Him; and His *is the most exalted state* in the heavens and the earth, and He is the Mighty, the Wise.

Section 4

Islam responds to Human Nature

38. Then give to the near of kin his due, and to the needy and the wayfarer; this is best for those who desire Allah's pleasure, and these it is who are successful.

39. And whatever you lay out at usury, so that it may increase in the property of men, it shall not increase with Allah; and whatever you give in charity, desiring Allah's pleasure—it is these (persons) that shall get manifold.

40. Allah is He Who created you, then gave you sustenance, then He causes you to die, then brings you to life. Is there any of your associate-gods who does aught of it? Glory be to Him, and exalted be He above what they associate (with Him).

Section 5

A Transformation

41. Corruption has appeared in the land and the sea on account of what the hands of men have wrought, that He may make them taste a part of that which they have done, so that they may return.

42. Say: Travel in the land, then see how was the end of those before: most of them were polytheists.

43. Then set *yourself* upright to the right *course* before there come from Allah the day which cannot be averted: on that day they shall become separated.

44. Whoever disbelieves, *he shall be responsible for* his disbelief, and whoever does good, they prepare (good) for their own souls.

48. Allah is He Who sends forth the winds so they raise a cloud, then He spreads it forth in the sky as He pleases, and He breaks it up so that you see the rain coming forth from inside it; then when He causes it to fall upon whom He pleases of His servants, lo! they are joyful;

49. Though they were before this, before it

was sent down upon them, confounded in sure despair.

50. Look then at the signs of Allah's mercy, how He gives life to the earth after its death, most surely He is the quickener of the dead; and He has power over all things.

CHAPTER XXXI

Section 2

Luqman's Advice to his Son

12. And certainly We gave wisdom to Luqman, saying: Be grateful to Allah. And whoever is grateful, he is only grateful for his own soul; and whoever is ungrateful, then surely Allah is Self-sufficient, Prai[illegible]

13. And when Luqman said to his son while he admonished him: O my son! do not associate aught with Allah; most surely polytheism is a grievous iniquity—

14. And We have enjoined man in respect of his parents—his mother bears him with faintings upon faintings and his weaning takes two years—saying: Be grateful to Me and to both *your* parents; to Me is the eventual coming.

15. And if they contend with *you* that *you should* associate with Me what *you have* no knowledge of, do not obey them, and keep company with them in this world kindly, and follow the

way of him who turns to Me, then to Me is your return, then will I inform you of what you did—

16. O my son! surely if it is the very weight of the grain of a mustard-seed, even though it is in (the heart of) rock, or (high above) in the heaven or (deep down) in the earth, Allah will bring it (to light); surely Allah is Knower of subtilties, Aware:

17. O my son! keep up prayer and enjoin the good and forbid the evil, and bear patiently that which befalls *you*; surely this is one of the affairs *earnestly enjoined*:

18. And do not turn *your* face away from people in contempt, nor go about in the land exulting overmuch: surely Allah does not love any self-conceited boaster:

19. And pursue the right course in *your* going about and lower *your* voice: surely the most hateful of voices is braying of the asses.

CHAPTER XLIX

Section 2

Respect for each Other

11. O you who believe! let not (one) people laugh at (another) people, perchance they may be better than they, nor let women (laugh) at (other) women, perchance they may be better than they; and do not find fault with your own people nor

call one another by nicknames; evil is a bad name after faith, and whoever does not turn, these it is that are the unjust.

12. O you who believe! avoid most of suspicion, for surely suspicion in some cases is a sin, and do not spy nor let some of you backbite others. Does one of you like to eat the flesh of his dead brother? But you abhor it; and be careful of (your duty to) Allah, surely Allah is Oft-returning (to mercy), Merciful.

15. The believers are only those who believe in Allah and His Apostle, then they doubt not and struggle hard with their wealth and their lives in the way of Allah; they are the truthful ones.

CHAPTER LVIII

Section 2

Secret Counsels condemned

10. Secret counsels are only (the work) of the devil that he may cause to grieve those who believe, and he cannot hurt them in the least except with Allah's permission; and on Allah let the believers rely.

THE WAY OF THE SUFI

"The definitive account of ancient Sufi teaching. A great many common Western distortions and misinterpretations are cleared away, and much valuable source material anthologized."

Tribune

"A present for anyone who, though religious, finds the current orthodoxies unpalatable."

Times Literary Supplement

"Highly educative, basic course of study; intrinsic relevance to all."

The Hindu

"A key book . . . can assist to demonstrate other possible uses of the mind . . . gives new material on method, history, personnel, much of it from oral sources."

The Observer

The Way of the Sufi
by Idries Shah
The Octagon Press

THE SPIRIT OF THE EAST

Today the kinship of all religious thought and dogma is becoming more apparent to mankind — and the value of Oriental thought to the Occidental mind is obvious. Here is a selection from Moslem, Parsee, Hindu, Hebrew, Confucian and other sources, chosen not only for their spiritual worth but also the particular virtues of each creed which they represent.

The aim of this book is to introduce readers to the religious thought of the East, which — for reasons of language and other difficulties — they might otherwise have considered inaccessible.

The Spirit of the East
Sirdar Ikbal Ali Shah
The Octagon Press

REFLECTIONS

This selection of Idries Shah's own fables, aphorisms and teachings is now in its third edition and continues to be extremely popular.

Pocket-sized, it is immensely entertaining and at the same time offers an alternative view of our society that is both refreshing and profitable.

'More wisdom that I have found in any other books this year'.

Pat Williams *Review of the Year, BBC.*

'It seems to oblige the mind to scorn the satisfaction of going from A to B in favour of an approach from a different angle, taking in unsuspected territory, hatches out as modified behaviour'.

Evening News

Reflections
by Idries Shah
The Octagon Press

TEACHINGS OF RUMI
THE MASNAVI

Jalaluddin Rumi's great work, *The Masnavi*, was 43 years in the writing. During the past seven hundred years, this book, called by Iranians 'The Koran in Persian', a tribute paid to no other book, has occupied a central place in Sufism.

'*The Masnavi* is full of profound mysteries, and a most important book in the study of Sufism — mysteries which must, for the most part, be left to the discernment of the reader.'

F. Hadland Davis

'To the Sufi, if not to anyone else, this book speaks from a different dimension, yet a dimension which is in a way within his deepest self'.

Idries Shah

'The greatest mystical poet of any age'.

Professor R. A. Nicolson

'It can well be argued that he is the supreme mystical poet of all mankind'.

Professor A. J. Arberry

Teachings of Rumi: The Masnavi
Abridged and translated by E. H. Whinfield.
Octagon Press